GROWING UP WITH...

By Nicky Weller, Barry Cain, Russell Reader & Den Davis

Copyright © 2017 Nicetime Productions

Book Compiled by:
Nicky Weller, Barry Cain, Russell Reader

Designed by Phil Dias at Karma Creative Ltd (www.karma-creative.co.uk)

Book sponsored by Mike Pickles (Entrepreneur and Boxman)
at The Really Useful Products Ltd, Unit 2, Network North, Foxbridge Way, Normanton, West Yorkshire, WF6 1TN.

Printed in the UK by s023

Thanks to: All our contributors for making this book possible,

The Karma Team - Phil, Nick & Pierre,
Pledge Music - Paul Dando, Jack D'Arcy, Malcolm Dunbar and Paul Barton.

ISBN - 978-0-9933127-1-7

Photographers:

Martyn Goddard , Jill Furmanovsky, Francesco Mellina, Virginia Turbett, Walt Davidson, Neil Matthews.

Published and Distributed by Nicetime Productions.

CONTENTS...

NEAT NEAT NEAT...

CAREER OPPORTUNITIES...

EVER FALLEN IN LOVE WITH SOMEONE...

INTRODUCTION...

Oh fuck, it's another book about punk.

Another slice of shit with a portion of shit on the side. Yep, I hold my hands up, this book is all that and more. Let's face it, it's got blatant cash-in written through it like a stick of Brighton rock.

Don't worry me none. Not since John Lennon died. I remember vividly. Tuesday morning. 9 December. 1980. The alarm radio, set for 7am, pumped out the news that he'd been shot and hurled me into consciousness. He was my idol. Nobody talked the talk and walked the walk like John Lennon. Fucking nobody. The consummate punk with granny glasses. Ok, apart from the first two solo albums, *Rock 'n' Roll* and a handful of singles - masterpieces all - his solo output was wafer thin and mainly shit. But I'd forgive Lennon anything because of the unmitigated joy and spunk he brought to the party of my youth.

So, I leapt out of bed and immediately began to ring those friends I knew would share my grief.

When I got to the office everyone was shell shocked. We'd just published the first issue of Flexipop! magazine with a little help from an East End company that specialised in printing soft core porn and one-off pop magazines - it's a long story. They wanted us, that's Tim Lott and myself, to bring out a regular pop mag and we, with a huge slug of foolhardiness, agreed. The phenomenally successful *Smash Hits* printed hit single lyrics so we went one better and featured actual unreleased flexi discs from top acts. We'd never published anything before and had been on a high since Flexipop! issue 1 hit the shelves. That morning's dreadful news had brought us back down to earth with a bang.

The door to the office slowly opened and a head poked round. It was the sales guy from the printer - an affable, charming wide-boy with a sharp eye for a deal as many truly successful men are.

" 'ere, 'ave you 'erd the news?' 'e asked.

"Terrible," we all said, in unison.

"Yeah," he said. "Let's get a fucking magazine out, quick."

I wrote *John Lennon: A Legend* that night with the help of a few old mags, books and comics knocking around at home, a chunk of sweet memories and a piece of my heart. The copy was at the typesetter 6am Wednesday morning and the mag was on the presses that night. It made some London shops by the weekend and was nationwide by the following Wednesday. We beat the *Melody Maker* John Lennon one-off mag to the streets by a week. Technology my arse.

It was 85p a throw and we sold a not too shabby 70,000 copies. I felt a little guilty at first but figured Johnny wouldn't mind. And, in a perverse way, writing that magazine gave me a sense of real contribution; that I was somehow personally involved in the whole process of his passing and consequently closer to the man and the artist. It also gave me enough dosh for a brand-new Suzuki jeep so it really was the best of both worlds.

I must admit, I'm not sure I would've involved myself in such a venture if I hadn't still been under a Malcolm McLaren spell. Through the late summer, early autumn of 1980, I interviewed Malcolm most nights at my flat for the purposes of his autobiography which he'd ask me to edit.

I defy anyone not to be contaminated by such a man after listening to his tales for nearly fifty hours. Producing *John Lennon: A Legend* had the smell of sleaze about it but, like the Pistols, it was well produced sleaze that a lot of people with the freedom of choice wanted. Like the Pistols it was a palatable sleaze because it continued to sell for months when the shelves were full of alternatives. Like the Pistols it was a punk sleaze because we did it ourselves. But only the Pistols had the artistic sleaze. Malcolm was the biggest chancer I ever met and believe me, I've met a few. But he could back it up with wit, imagination and an element of despair that made him the affable, charming wide-boy with a sharp eye for a deal as many truly successful men are. The one difference with Malcolm, his wide-boy was more wide-eyed boy.

Incidentally, the autobiography still hasn't seen the light of day due to the complications of contracts and it will be tragedy if those lost tapes of punk are never heard.

This book is no different from *John Lennon: A Legend* except there's no jeep at the end and you hope enough will be sold to cover your costs and time and effort, though the chance of that is pretty remote. As a result, the sleaze factor has rescinded considerably but the feeling of contribution is more intense because punk in Britain in 1977 meant everything to me and, to use a well-worn phrase, changed my life. Books like these are now labours of love. But labours of love are better than no labours at all, especially when you reach a certain age and the world keeps repeating itself over and over again until it has nothing left to offer. Trouble is, that certain age can be any age, any fucking age at all. Back in '77, life was repeating itself over and over again for far too many teenagers. The shock of punk knocked that repetition out of sync, like a heart with atrial fibrillation. You can live with it for a while but it'll get you in the end.

The palpitations, however, are some kind of wonderful.

Punk may have started in '76 but it mattered in '77, the year of the debut. Debut albums like *Never Mind The Bollocks*, *The Clash*, *Damned Damned Damned*, *In The City*, *Rattus Norvegicus*; debut singles like 'White Riot', 'Grip', 'In The City', 'Oh Bondage Up Yours'; debut trips on planes to faraway places, debut thoughts, dreams, passions, debut everything. A beautiful, debut flame that lit up the teenage blue suburban skies.

A generation could dream again thanks to discordant sulphate speed guitars and vindictive voices. For many that dream has lasted a lifetime and acquired a tenacity of Barry White never-gonna-give-you up proportions.

An army of punks can be seen never giving it up at the truly magical Rebellion Festival held every summer in the warm glow of the Blackpool Winter Gardens. I must admit, I was a little perturbed at the thought of thousands of beer-bellied, middle-aged punks sporting rapidly thinning Mohicans and heavily tattooed arms clutching portly Poly Urethanes and bouncing up and down on happy slapping folds of fat to the UK Subs.

But, like this book, appearances can be deceptive. The four-day Rebellion Festival is an uplifting occasion packed with great bands, terrific food, markets of intriguing stalls, art, literature and a sense of belonging. And everybody looks fucking amazing. Punk is still soaked in style. The folds of fat were figments of my tired imagination, an imagination that obviously needs revving up occasionally.

And then there's the music at Rebellion. Swathes of sonic sex booming down from stage after stage, songs sculpted by bands playing to the biggest audiences of their lives alongside bands playing to the biggest lives of their audience. It's a truly joyous occasion and a privilege to be part of it.

It's also tinged with sadness, for me anyway. Selfish really, but it's simply the realisation that I'm not the immortal being I always thought I was, that time is passing by at an alarming rate and swallowing up the future. If Rebellion had been held in 1977, the average age of the audience would've been about 21, if not younger. Now it's nearer 50, if not older. The event does attract a sizeable amount of people under thirty but it's still essentially a bunch of middle-aged people listening and jumping to middle-aged music, a music that now packs a bigger kick in the nostalgia bollocks than the political ones. And so it should. This is the soundtrack to their teenage wastelands. The thousands of fans that pack out the tantalisingly cavernous Winter Gardens are the people that grew up with punk, that shaped it, revelled in it, never let it out of their sight and made it more potent than a fifties' Elvis. The greatest pop there ever was and ever will be.

Every generation has its own music, we just got lucky I guess. I defy anyone to find a more exciting, inspiring or dangerous year in the history of pop than 1977. It was all downhill after as music was slowly poisoned by endless technology piss-shit designed to sublimate the sound to the vision. Pop music lost its ability to incite and delight the youth of the world and is now, with few exceptions, computer game muzak or a box set boogie or TV talent show fodder or videos where the interpretation of the music is determined for you by making the image, their

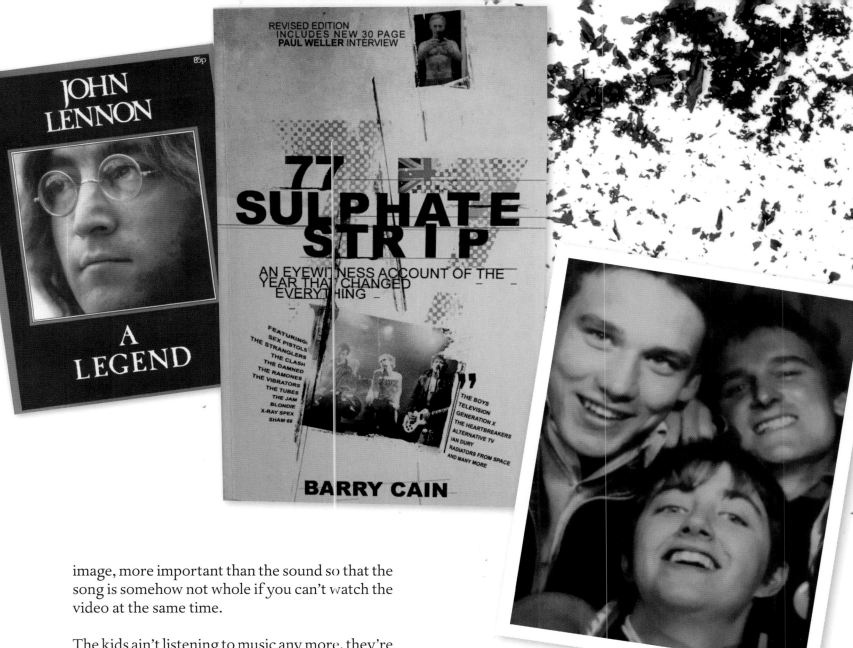

image, more important than the sound so that the song is somehow not whole if you can't watch the video at the same time.

The kids ain't listening to music any more, they're fucking seeing it.

I started out as a music writer on *Record Mirror* in November 1976 and two weeks later found myself sitting opposite Johnny Rotten at EMI, interviewing him on the eve of the Bill Grundy debacle. Just got lucky I guess. That set the scene for the year ahead during which I was fortunate enough to go on the road with the Pistols, Clash, Jam, Damned, Stranglers, Heartbreakers and Demis Roussos. I saw and did things I never dreamed possible and was happy to be an island in the sun in the RM offices above Covent Garden tube station. I thought it would last forever and ever and it's taken a while to realise nothing ever does.

Not even Demis...

So yes, this is indeed, another fucking book about punk. And I'm very proud to say it. Oh bondage up yours, you fuckin' rotters...

– Barry Cain 2017

One of my clearest punk memories was being 15 and seeing Adam Ant at the Vortex, I think it was October 1977... he was supporting Siouxsie and the Banshees. I remember him coming onto the stage with Jordan... before he was a pirate... he was into bondage.. and a raincoat, it was a real eye opener for me.. let alone the audience in rubber!

I also remember going to the Roxy club .. to see the Nipple erectors, Shane was hilarious chucking flowers around the stage like Morrissey... then he poured a pint of lager over Shanne who played bass... I don't think anyone could believe it didn't all blow up. I loved the Roxy it was such a great little club...i went a few times when The Jam played there... I used to sell Jam badges for 10p...

Happy days...

– Nicky Weller 2017

I wasn't disaffected was I?

I guess I was a 'head in the clouds'-accept-the-situation type of youth. I was brought up on The Beatles and the Stones. Dylan was a Sunday favourite in our house.

My older bro, Terry, used to bring home good stuff - Motown albums, reggae etc until he grew his hair long and the music got heavier.

Glam was big when I was at school and I loved Bowie and Bolan but never really got into Roxy Music. Someone said I should be listening to this and he handed me *Dark Side Of The Moon.* I listened, and it went straight over my head.

By that time, bands seemed untouchable, flying in privately owned jets and driving about in limos. This led me to believe for a long time that you had to be a really special person or very lucky to go to a concert.

And all the time the music was getting more pompous - there's gotta be a record out there somewhere from the seventies of someone farting into a trumpet!

Then one weekend in the winter of '76, I happened to watch the London Weekend Show with Janet St Porter reporting about 'Punk'.

I can't remember too much about it other than it featured a band called the Sex Pistols with a singer called Johhny Rotten talking about how he, "didn't 'ave any 'eroes, they're all useless." I was 17 and immediately wanted to know more. I bought 'New Rose' followed by 'Anarchy In The UK' (I got stared at by shoppers in Wembley market when the record stallholder called to his mate, "We got any of those Sex Pistols records, 'Arry?")

'77 came round and we were suddenly flooded with singles and albums by The Clash, Damned, Jam etc and the picture sleeve made a big comeback too which was great. The albums were raw and fast, the songs played at 100 miles an hour.

I didn't want to believe what the music press were saying about the influences coming from the USA with bands like The Stooges and New York Dolls, even though The Pistols were playing 'No Fun'! I thought, this is all ours, not theirs!

It was Jubilee Year and I loved the fact 'God Save The Queen' got banned by the Beeb. Me and a mate went on a bit of a pub crawl on the day of the celebration and it was noticeable how many jukeboxes were playing punk stuff.

I still wasn't really a gig goer. Me and a couple of mates went down to Brunel University to try to get into The Pistols gig that Joe Corre mentions in this book. But there was no chance.

I was more of a clubber and adopted the 'soul boy' look. I always felt there was a bit of a crossover with that look and Punk. I'm not talking about bin liners, chains and safety pins, but The Smiths Carpenter jeans adopted by the soul boys. I had red, green and black pairs that were almost like watered-down bondage trousers. I also sported plastic sandals or Converse and a mohair jumper (my auntie knitted mine). I thought my style represented both looks.

The Kings Road was the place to be on a Saturday in the seventies. You'd arrive late morning, browse the record and clothes shops and then go off to Stamford Bridge in the afternoon.

Though a lot of people did, I never felt the desire to pick up a guitar and get on stage but I wanted to be involved. A couple of years later I got a job at Nomis Rehearsal Studios and from there went on the road and worked with various bands over the coming years.

So you could say, Punk really did change my life.

— *Russell Reader 2017*

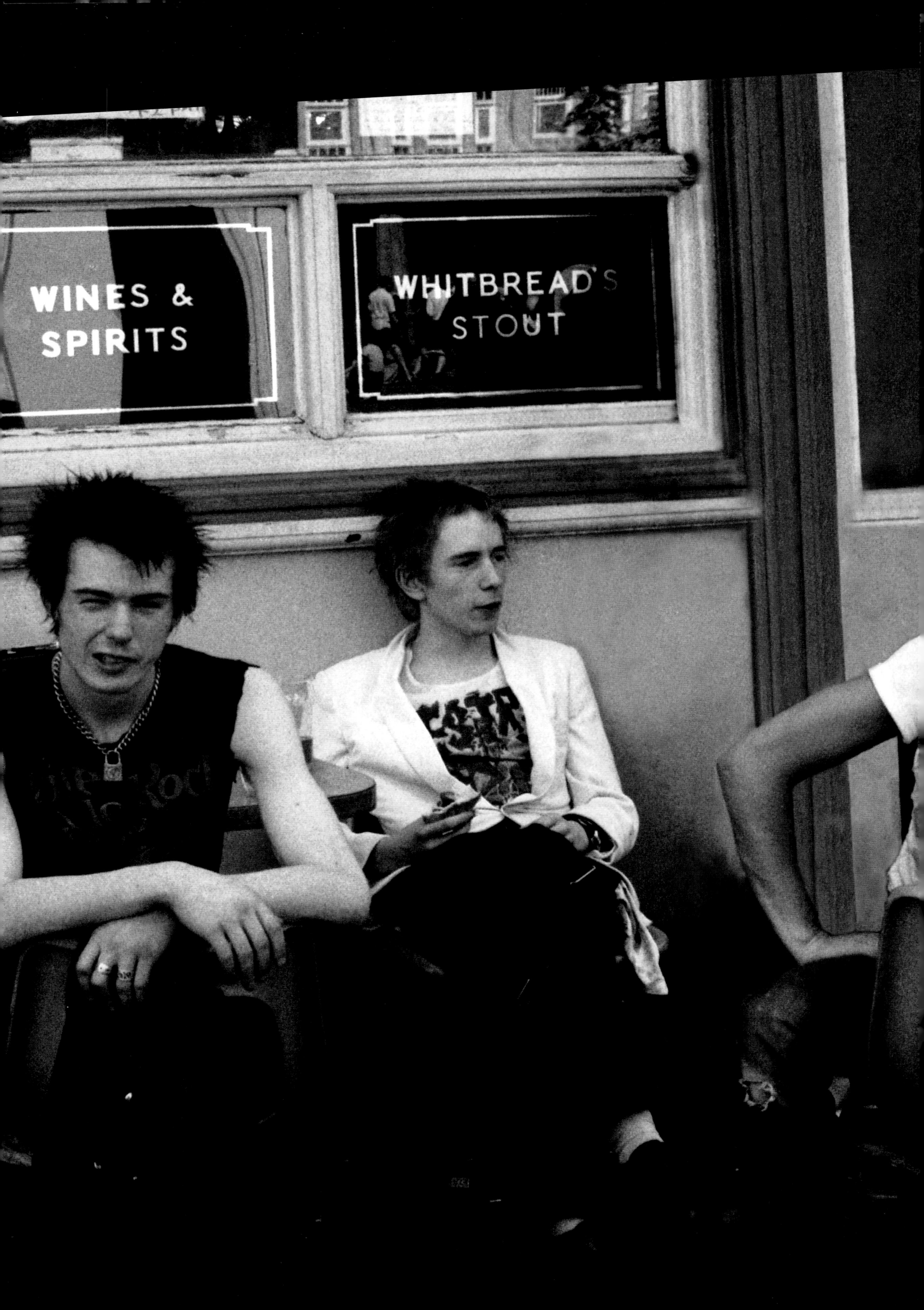
WINES & SPIRITS
WHITBREAD'S STOUT

NEVER MIND THE BOLLOCKS...

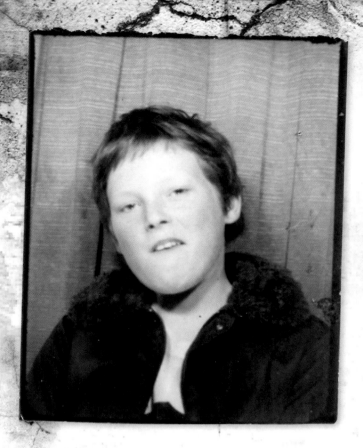

JOE CORRE

16 December 1977, Brunel University – one of the last gigs the Sex Pistols played in the UK before heading off to the US. I'd just turned 11 and my mother took me to that gig because she thought it might be the last chance I'd get to see them perform. She and Malcolm sensed that the band were on the verge of self-destruction.

I'd never seen the Pistols play before and they were incredible. I was in awe of the band and their sound. The show took place in a big sports hall and we were standing in a viewing gallery halfway up one of the walls. The whole place went nuts and turned into a sea of pogoing kids. I can still feel the hairs standing up on the back of my neck.

After the gig, I sat on a chair upstairs and felt something jabbing into the back of my head. I turned around and there was Nancy Spungen stabbing her stiletto heels into me for no apparent reason. I remember vividly Steve Jones was there scoffing a load of bananas – he was putting on a lot of weight at that time – as he wiped off the gob that always covered his clothes when he came offstage.

I loved Steve. The first time he came into the shop he nicked a pair of trousers and Malcolm chased him down the street. He caught him but they ended up liking each other and he started working for Malcolm as a driver. He was round our flat all the time and I saw a lot of him before the Pistols started.

Steve's mate used to work at Watney's brewery in Wandsworth. In the early days when the band were due to play a gig, Steve and Paul would go see their mate and nick loads of beer. On the way, they'd pick up my brother, Ben, and me and make us act as lookouts while they were taking the booze.

Steve was always stealing cars. Every car he ever had then was nicked. When you got in the back seat of one of his motors there were all these fucking knickers stuffed down the sides of the seats. He'd shag girls in the car and keep their knickers. I'd hold them up to him and ask what they were and he'd just say, "Don't worry about it, Joe."

Mum sent me to this school in Chelsea because she wanted me to have more 'cultural' influences. I used to wear a red blazer, shorts, sandals and a little cap and had to learn ballet and the recorder and French. At the end of each school day the headmistress, who was called Mrs Whitehead, used to stand by the door and all the kids would form a queue and the boys would bow and the girls would curtsey as we said, "Good afternoon Mrs Whitehead." The Pistols used to pick me up from that school and when it was my turn to bow, I was as red as a fucking beetroot because the band would stand there taking the piss and roll up laughing as they shouted, "Good afternoon Mrs Blackhead."

I haven't spoken to Steve for over ten years. When I was about to burn the Punk stuff, he did finally get in touch through social media. "Don't burn it, Joe," he said. "Give it to me. What do you want to burn all that clobber for?"

I used to see Sid a lot too. I remember one day in '77, Mum and I took him to the dentist in Streatham. In the car on the way back, Sid was pleading with Vivienne, "Please don't take me back to Nancy. I don't want to see her, I can't see her. Please don't take me back." He felt so trapped in that relationship. Sid was such a complicated guy.

I was never very close to John. I didn't get the impression that he liked me, probably because he had such a strained relationship with Malcolm.

What stands out about 1977 for me was the Jubilee. There were loads of street parties and everyone seemed to be wrapping bog rolls round lampposts. I thought those celebrations had nothing to do with us – we were so far apart from all that. There was this huge outpouring of patriotism while the papers were busy whipping up hatred with fabricated stories of vile, obscene Punks spitting and swearing across the country.

As a result, you took your life in your hands just walking around in Punk clothes. I was the Pistols number one fan and used to make all my own badges and Mum used to cut my hair in little squares like a tiled roof. My school blazer was covered in Pistols memorabilia and I wore bondage trousers and boots. I always had a Seditionaries' T shirt under my school shirt and was regularly sent home when the teachers discovered it. They were my clothes and I loved them but when I walked around dressed like that, grown men would come up to me in the street and spit in my face – I was ten for fucksake.

That whole Jubilee joke came to a head for me with the Pistols boat trip up the Thames. I stayed at home with my brother and Vivienne and Malcolm didn't return that night because they'd been arrested. I remember getting up in the morning and there was nobody there. We didn't know what to do; it was so weird.

Vivienne was no stranger to run-ins with the law. The police were constantly raiding her shop and confiscating anything that said 'fuck' on it. She'd keep replenishing the shelves with more T shirts and the police would keep coming back and take them away again. She and Malcolm were eventually charged with displaying indecent items and the main culprit was the cowboys' T shirt. The judge ruled that the cowboys' penises were nearly touching so that made it indecent. And one of the cowboys was straightening the other's necktie so he decided that was indecent as well!

The shop was always being smashed up, usually by Chelsea fans. It was such a glamourous looking frontage with white frosted glass windows and a Seditionaries' gold plaque on the door. But in no time, it looked like a fucking barricade. On one occasion, Vivienne broke her finger while trying to hold back the baying thugs as they pushed against the door.

At the time, we were living in a flat in Clapham and it was like a garment factory. The bathroom was the dyeing department, the kitchen the printing department and the hallway was full up with fabrics. The Hells Angels used to come around to do the leather work and studding. It was pandemonium.

On top of that, we used to have terrible infestations of cockroaches because of the common central heating system for the whole block. There was a big boiler at the back of the flats and the cockroaches used to crawl along the heating pipes into the flats. If you went into the kitchen at night and turned on the light, the roaches would dash for cover. Malcolm was so squeamish and neurotic and he'd be screaming like a big girl and stamping on them in his bare feet and there'd be this squashed purple goo all over the fucking floor.

We had a phone installed at the flat for the first time in '77 and Malcolm said to Ben and me, "If anyone rings, pick it up and say, 'Malcolm McLaren's office'." How could he possibly think that was believable? It was so childish, but that's how he was.

As soon as we got the phone connected, the death threats started. I'd pick it up and hear a creepy voice, "We're gonna come and kill you and burn your house down."

By far the worst experience of '77 for me was the time the National Front surrounded our flat and threw a brick through the window and stuck turds through the letterbox. For some reason, we never had any curtains and because we lived on the first floor you could see in from the street.

The NF started banging on the front door and my brother and I looked out of the window and saw a jeering mob. But the really upsetting thing for me was that standing alongside the NF supporters were all our mates. They were mostly kids from immigrant families – Jamaicans, Sri Lankans, Pakistanis – that we always knocked around with, and there they were laughing and throwing bangers and stones at our window. It meant even our friends hated us and treated us as the enemy.

I remember Malcolm saying, "Turn out the lights and pretend we're not in." How the fuck do you turn the lights out and then pretend you're not in? We all huddled together in the hallway as the yobs were screaming through the letterbox. It was terrifying.

So, what I mostly remember about '77 was the aggro and the grief and Mum getting arrested and me being regularly taken out of my bed in the middle of the night and going to my gran's because Vivienne thought the police were going to come around.

My view of Punk is very different from other people's and I guess that contributed to the burn up I did last year. For the establishment to now embrace Punk smacks of hypocrisy. If you want to take a trip down memory lane it better be the right fucking trip. Tell it like it really was – not all this 'we're all Punkers now' bullshit. We were hated and vilified – the Pistols were banned from playing, you couldn't hear them on the radio, couldn't buy their records. And when they did make it to number one, we were told there's no fucking number one that week. That's how much they were afraid of you.

You can't do all that and now, all these years later, say Punk is part of British culture. Okay, maybe it is, but you better fucking say what side of the fence you were on at the time.

The worst aspect of Punk was the way it was used to sell young people the idea that living a Punk lifestyle was going to solve their problems. It never was and that to me was its failure. If you're going to be anti-establishment, if you're going to say we don't respect your morals or your taboos, well you better have something alternative to offer. You must be able to say, "We don't like this, but we want this."

Just saying you want anarchy is not enough. There's nowhere to go if you can't come up with an alternative. That's why Punk could be nothing more than a marketing exercise. Don't try and tell people that it's going change your life and offer solutions because all that's being offered is another illusion.

A *Never Mind The Bollocks* credit card is still a fucking credit card. It's just an illusion and I'm not buying it. I don't need your fucking marketing bollocks because my experience of Punk was something entirely different. Punk was about standing up and saying we're gonna try and change things, we're dangerous and you better take care, you better look at this.

Where Punk did succeed was that it freed some people from their mental shackles. It gave them the confidence to say, "Do you know what, I can do something else. I can be a musician, I can be an artist, I can be a fashion designer. I don't have to go to the careers' office and take the fucking role that's pushed onto me. I don't have to go and work down the coal mine, I don't have to go and work in the pie shop. I can choose what I want to do.

Once you can get up on stage in front of people and not give a fuck about how you sound, then getting on that stage again is easy. That confidence can then be used in any situation you choose. You could begin to believe in another possibility, an alternative.

Even by as early as 1978, Punk had become a fucking tourist attraction and that's years before credit card Punk and McDonalds Punk and beer Punk. Do you know, a company now owns the copyright on the word 'Punk' when it's used on any beer related product? Some geezer was sued the other day because he wanted to open a bar called Draught Punk. How fucking ridiculous is that?

That's what I've been trying to demonstrate by burning the Punk memorabilia. It's an opportunity to divert attention to far more serious matters that concern me like climate change, the extinction of the species, the annihilation of the planet.

ANARCHY IN THE UK...

The Artists...

ANDY RADWAN

I continued juggling the trials and tribulations of school life and Eater's continued ascent from local boys making good to low-rent punk rock stars.

The band's growing popularity gave Brian, Dee and me the confidence and freedom to continue our double lives as schoolboys by day and grown-ups by night. A major hassle was having to get up early and go to school after a late night out. I was forever going about my day in a hazy, happy fog, like a bubble, pleasantly shielded from my environment. I wasn't so worried about missing school anymore. I wouldn't have bothered going at all, if it hadn't been for the threat of my mum being taken to court. When he wasn't writing heavy handed letters to the LEA, the Head had taken to giving me a wide berth around the school. I hadn't been caned for ages, despite a variety of spank-able offences. He didn't seem to know what to do with me. On one hand, he wanted to see out my expulsion from the school, whilst on the other hand, he wanted to keep his distance. I think I made him nervous. For the time being, though, Eater were moving forwards, unhindered.

We now had a record deal on the table with Dave Goodman's label – Rotten Records, a record company he was about to launch with Johnny Rotten, no less. Johnny Rotten, as in The Sex Pistols – as in the most important group in the universe.

Unless Dave was having us on, this was the golden opportunity that every would-be pop star dreams of – being signed to a label owned by your idol. How lucky were we?

Dave Goodman had invited Brian and me to a gig by a new band called, rather un-inspiringly for a London band, Chelsea. Like with every new group pledging allegiance to the cause, interest was generated by word of mouth by virtue of who they knew and who managed them.

A showcase gig like this was also a great excuse for a 'Punk Happening' – a tag that could be applied to each and every punk gig at the time due to lack of bands.

Which was why we were able to draw such a good crowd to our self-arranged gig at Finchley Manor Hill school with The Damned despite the lack of publicity or the badly thought out logistics, being several miles away from the nearest tube station, etc. Any excuse to get out there and mingle, was a chance not to be missed.

Dave Goodman had seen Jonh Ingham's piece on 'The A-Z of Punk Rock', including the profile he'd written about Eater, after meeting us at the Windmill Studio rehearsal – the time Rat Scabies had been there. Dave's immediate offer of a deal, before even hearing us, had me suspicious, but as The Pistols sound man, he was well placed to start a label, and to produce the bands. Rotten, according to Dave, would be "Head of A&R" – meaning he got to choose the bands they signed.

It followed then, that Goodman must have played him the demo we'd recorded in his shed, with polystyrene drums. How Johnny Rotten could have been impressed by that, I wasn't sure, but neither was I going to ask too many questions.

"Andy man," said Dave, "now The Pistols have been dropped by EMI, this is your chance to get a single out before them. I mean, The Damned have beaten everyone to it already, but if we get a move on, like get you into the studio ASAP, Eater could be the second."

Dave wanted to make us hurry up and sign on his contract's dotted line. I didn't see the importance of getting a record out before The Pistols – or anyone else come to that. The very fact we were discussing releasing an Eater record at all was enough. It all seemed so wonderfully crazy it was almost too good to be true. Having already experienced the upset broken promises tend to instigate, I couldn't afford to get my hopes up, not least because I'd never be able to live it down, telling all and sundry we had a deal with Johnny Rotten, only for it to be proven false. We had to verify things ourselves, that was all there was to it, Brian and I were in agreement about that, even if it meant bursting our own bubble, which was something we really didn't like to do.

So, when the opportunity to ask the man himself

EATER

on record
their new debut album
THE ALBUM TLR LP 001

hear how good it is
before your'e told!!

also their great new
single LOCK IT UP TLR 004
still available
OUTSIDE VIEW TLR 001
THINKING OF THE USA TLR 003

Distributed by The Label Records 01-385 6012

arrived, we had no choice but to jump on it.

"Will the Pistols definitely be there tonight?" I asked, not wanting to seem as though I was making too much of an issue out of it, or that I didn't believe him.

"Bound to be. I just spoke to Paul and Steve and they're going," Dave responded, sounding sure of himself, but with a hint of reluctance. He'd been so encouraging and so full of flattery, it seemed wrong to treat him with any suspicion at all. There was no point in taking this any further, though, not yet. The first thing to do was speak to Johnny Rotten himself, get it direct from the horse's mouth, something that Goodman was maybe gambling on us not doing. He must have considered the potential embarrassment, probably arriving at the conclusion that neither Brian nor I would have the courage to actually go and ask him. He underestimated us, not that it made much difference in the end.

The ICA was full, and despite the cold night, it was uncomfortably hot inside, which might have had something to do with the extra weight I was carrying. I'd taken to keeping my pyjamas on underneath my clothes since the summer

had passed. Not only did it save time in the morning rush to get to school, but it was also a good way of keeping warm now that Autumn was in the air. It made going for a piss a bit more complicated than it should've been, but there were distinct advantages to wearing your PJ's under your clothes. Quite often I had no idea where I'd be sleeping on any given night, making the convenience of ever ready PJ's a real plus. There was one small drawback to wearing the extra padding, although it kept me warm outside, it made for an uncomfortable evening when crammed into a hot and sweaty club like now. It also left me open to embarrassment, should anyone discover my secret. Wearing pyjamas out wasn't the coolest of things to do.

Chelsea were managed by a guy called John Krevine, who owned a shop on the Kings Rd, producing his own line in punky clothes, essentially a knocked-up version of Malcolm's shop's designs. Both were within yards of each other, but you couldn't really say they were in competition. They may have made zippered trousers, Day-Glo socks and shirts with paint on them more affordable, but everyone knew where the good stuff came from. The dangers of a band having a manager who owned a clothes shop were

obvious. Getting all dressed up in a shop's latest range doesn't sound very rock 'n' roll, but theirs was a unique arrangement. Vivienne's designs were by no means uniform. The stereotype punk sporting a green Mohican, tattoos, body piercings and studded leather jackets, came long after the scene was already over. The Pistols looked cool no matter what they wore.

On the downside, the clothing connection handed ammunition to the critics, with the accusation that the Sex Pistols were nothing more than talentless models, dressed up in their manager's clothes, flogging not only his wares, but his self-indulgent political ideas too. To a hackneyed old music journalist, it was nothing new; bored, middle aged business men with a few quid to spare, throwing their lot in behind a band, adding pop group to their list of acquisitions. There are many examples of successful partnerships – Andrew Loog Oldham/The Stones, Brain Epstein/The Beatles, Elvis/Col.Tom, Tony Wilson/Happy Mondays, etc – but there are a hundred more for each one that fucks up before even reaching the starting post. What ties all of them together, successful or not, is the absolute, 100 per cent certainty the union will end in tears for both manager and band.

After Chelsea divided in two, Gene October remained loyal to Krevine, whilst Billy Idol, Tony James and John Towe were scooped up by Krevine's accountant – a guy with a gold tooth who, noticing the brisk business in 'punk stuff',

decided to open the first Punk rock club – the infamous Roxy. It was a shrewd move on both sides and all of it incidental. In that moment, upon the ever-shifting sands that we stood, Chelsea Mk 1, were pretty cool. The applause in between songs was noticeably muted for such a packed venue, but being their first gig, I figured they didn't really have any fans yet. I knew how that felt. I only wished Eater's debut had been packed out with uninterested, cool people like this crowd of freaks.

Punk gigs were few and far between at the beginning, which meant that at every gig, whoever the band, and just by virtue of being a punk 'happening', it was assumed that anyone who was anyone within the ranks would be in attendance. Sure enough, they were all here tonight: The Clash, The Pistols, The Damned, Subway Sect, Malcolm McLaren, Jake Riviera, Chris Spedding and his long-time German heiress-girlfriend Nora Forster. People were getting drunk, making deals, comparing jackets and taking drugs in the toilet. The Government had made no secret of their distaste for the cultural threat posed by the Sex Pistols and their 'Anarchy In The UK' shtick. Malcolm McLaren and his situationist fun and games had no place in seventies Britain.
This could have been the perfect opportunity to once and for all put an end to the rabble-rousing phenomenon known as Punk Rock. One 'proper' Punk explosion later (pin it on the IRA) and everyone could sleep tight at night again.
RIP filth and fury.

ANDY MCCLUSKEY

I had a rather ambivalent attitude to Punk music as I had already discovered my alternative musical future in 1975 in the German import rack at Probe Records in Liverpool. As a teenager desperate to create a new and individual identity for myself, I had already found my escape from the cheesy disco pop and cliché ridden rock of the seventies. I would, however, explore every possible new musical avenue.

I bought all the Sex Pistols singles and 'White Riot' by The Clash and really fed off the energy and simplicity. But I was more interested in bands who were deconstructing the traditional rock song format; so I preferred things like 'Marquee Moon' by Television, 'Whole Wide World' by Wreckless Eric, 'Mongoloid' by Devo, and 'Psycho Killer' by Talking Heads. For me, the importance was in challenging the musical convention as much as an angry performance with the same old instruments.

The limitation of Punk for me was the use of the conventional rock instrument line-up of guitar, bass and drums. I was looking for a new sound as well as a new ethos. Punk's look and attitude was different, but the sound was actually just a simplified rock format. However, very quickly Paul Humphreys and I realized that we were essentially adopting one key element of Punk – grab any old cheap instrument, don't learn to play 'properly'…just start writing something simple and idiosyncratic. Synth Punk.

Since most of our friends were still into seventies prog rock we confined ourselves to the hobby of writing music in the back room of Paul's mother's house until hearing 'Warm Leatherette' by The Normal at Eric's club in Liverpool in the Summer of '78. This was the seminal Electro Punk recording by Daniel Miller. Garage Synth! We decided to dare to play our minimal synth music live for one gig only just to say that we had! Orchestral Manoeuvres in the Dark was created for that one off gig!

BILLY BRAGG

1977: bliss was it in that dawn to be 19 years-old! Me and my mates had been playing Stones' and Faces' songs in my parents' backroom for several years with no idea about how we might ever get a gig, never mind make a record. The rock stars of the day seemed so far away – across the other side of the stadium when we went to see The Who at Charlton or living the high life in LA having given up on England like Rod Stewart. The change when it came was sudden, like a tsunami that swept away everything in its path.

How did the news reach us? Was it when The Pistols swore on TV? When we saw The Jam at the Nashville Rooms? They certainly grabbed our attention but it was when we followed them to the Finsbury Park Rainbow weeks later when they opened for The Clash that the penny dropped: those guys on stage are the same age as me – if they can do it, so can I. Within a couple of weeks, I'd cut my hair, ditched the flares and started writing fast, punchy songs. By the end of the year, our little band had played at the Marquee Club in London and cut an EP for Chiswick Records.

Punk empowered us, telling kids to create their own culture rather than waiting around for something to happen. That DIY attitude still drives my creative impulses.

At the Roxy Club, Neal St Covent Garden, London this Saturday the 15th of January.

BILLY IDOL

Living in a world where a 'nothingness', 'a void', 'a hopelessness' existed; feeling as if life was passing you by with no way to effect a change. Seeing the Sex Pistols at the 100 Club on Oxford Street, with my Bromley Contingent mates one evening in early '76, showed me the answer to all the negativity... "Do what you love most" was the clarion call.

England, for us, was a soulless world of few possibilities but the Sex Pistols would change that and serve as our flagship. We were young and idealistic! Now it was up to us to start our own bands following Johnny Rotten's example of how to make the ordinary extraordinary. A few more bands started cropping up and I responded to a small ad in Melody Maker placed by Tony James and together we formed our own band, Generation X. It was great to know more people who cared about Punk music.

A growing perception among club owners that Punk shows were violent and to be avoided led us to look for and find a place to play we could call our own. The Roxy opened at the end of 1976 and was to feature shows by Siouxsie and the Banshees The Clash, Johnny Thunders Heartbreakers, Generation X, Slaughter and the Dogs and many others.

The club swam in flotsam, jetsam and various and sundry bodily fluids in between... every kind of activity went on in each corner of the club. People lived out the novel experience of being part of the London Punk scene, many bringing their own personally created lifestyle and fashion choices to this violent playground in the heart of Covent Garden. Leather jackets and spiky hair for guys; girls in mini-skirts, men's shirts as dresses, with a tie worn loosely at the neck, bondage leather wristbands, garish facial make-up, crazy coloured hair teased into formidable shapes when not hacked off, and towering fuck-me pumps on their feet to finish the overall effect.

In 1977, the Punk scene would grow in leaps and bounds, with ten becoming 20 and then 100. We were young and idealistic! We believed in the healing power of music and its ability to challenge society. We felt this new world should express the full range of emotions. Some, like myself, loved music and wanted to contribute that way. But others picked up a camera and became photographers or started a fanzine to become a journalists and talked about the scene we were in. The magic of Punk—or its blessing—was that nobody really knew what it was, exactly.

"If this was just about music, it would have been dead a long time ago." Malcom McClaren,

DEBBIE HARRY

I only know that at that time we were pretty much on the road all the time and promoting albums which is what all the bands wanted to do from the start. Although we didn't know jack about the business, and we made a lot of mistakes, we truly had the 'punk' spirit about fighting for it and being as abrasive as possible. Mostly we were thought of as more of a pop band or punk pop by this time as we had refined our sound somewhat.

BOZ BOORER

My first punk show was the Adverts at the Roundhouse in Sept '77. It was like a baptism into a new faith, from opening acts Johnny Moped through ATV and the Electric Chairs, I was mesmerized, I was a regular at the local record shop going through all the new arrivals sampling such delights as Slaughter and the Dogs and The Clash, then I was never the same after the Siouxsie and the Banshees show shortly later with Penetration, The Worst and The Buzzcocks or was it Spizz Oil? I was hungry for knowledge and an eager student after my earlier education through rockabilly and glam rock. It was such a huge revelation, I never looked back.

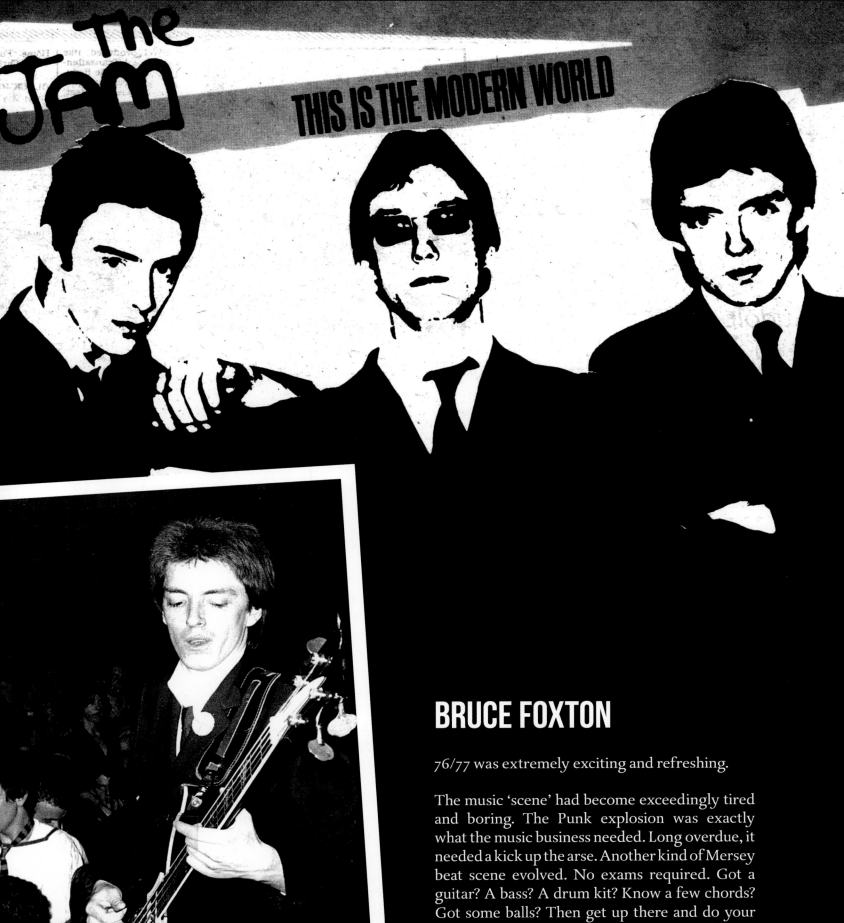

THE JAM

THIS IS THE MODERN WORLD

BRUCE FOXTON

76/77 was extremely exciting and refreshing.

The music 'scene' had become exceedingly tired and boring. The Punk explosion was exactly what the music business needed. Long overdue, it needed a kick up the arse. Another kind of Mersey beat scene evolved. No exams required. Got a guitar? A bass? A drum kit? Know a few chords? Got some balls? Then get up there and do your thing! Unfortunately, it wasn't long until fashion took over. It all got taken over by designers and everyone started wearing the same thing.

Nevertheless, some fantastic, original bands and songs came out of it. Some have gone but the music remains, as fresh as it was all those years ago.

God Save The Queen.

DAMNED

CAPTAIN SENSIBLE

A high point for me in 1977 was getting the opportunity to travel. Back then, international travel was still very much the domain of posh folks, apart from cheap package holidays to Spain and the like. It was wonderful to connect with our European neighbours, we're all the same after all. Nations mean very little in the grand scheme of things.

During one of our many jaunts abroad, I think it was in Holland, our manager Jake Riviera came up with the idea that Wayne County and me should get married! I guess it was for PR reasons. Alas, it never happened - we could've had the first 'rainbow' wedding.

On that same tour, I remember Sting was thrown out of our dressing room by Brian James after he asked for a bottle of wine. Brian told him he could have as much booze as he wanted when his band were headlining, but. "As you're now on the bottom rung of the ladder it shows me that you need to work a bit harder on your act." I wonder whatever happened to Sting?

In another country, the class of '77 would be national heroes. In the UK however, I get the impression Punk is a dirty little secret that would be better brushed under the carpet. I base that opinion on the fact that The Damned, and the other bands from then, get hardly any airplay. You've got to be a 'pretend' American Punk band on a big label to get on the playlists here.

What I liked about the UK bands in '77 was that they all sounded very different from each other. A lot of them had seen The Ramones at Dingwalls on 4 July 1976 and inspired them to kickstart their own scene. I mean, The Stranglers sounded nothing like The Buzzcocks and The Buzzcocks sounded nothing like The Clash. It was time for the likes of ELP and Yes to fuck right off and take their songs about elves and wizards with them.

Punk saved my arse. I had a shit education and the future looked bleak, stuffed with dead-end jobs and no hope. Before The Damned came along, I was dossing in a Brighton squat surrounded by junkies. Punk empowered me because it gave me the confidence to do it myself.

Punk was a glorious working class rebellion and that's why I disagreed with McLaren and his Bromley snobs at the time.

Damned, Damned, Damned was the first UK Punk album when it was released in February 1977 and it was basically us playing our 35-minute set over and over for two days until Nick Lowe was happy with it. There are hardly any overdubs or layering and I believe it faithfully captures the essence of Punk rock. I really believed we'd only ever make one album and as my face wasn't visible on the album sleeve, I nipped out and got a passport photo for the art designer to glue on somewhere. It's still on the back and people are always asking about that.

Punk was all about no stars, no heroes. I don't ask my plumber or postman for an autograph. I'm nothing special. Anyone can go out and buy a guitar and learn to make music.

SNIFFIN' GLUE...
AND OTHER ROCK'N'ROLL HABITS,
FOR ~~PUNKS~~ GIRLS! ③ SEPTEMBER '76.

THE MAG THAT DOESN'T LIKE GIVING YOU 'UP TO DATE' NEWS ON THE MUSIC SCENE. PRICE-25pence.

DAMNED

THE DAMNED ☆ SEX PISTOLS ☆ IGGY POP +
WITH

CARL HUNTER

Bootle in the late seventies meant three channels on a black and white television and no central heating. Who cared? I had a record player and a Schofield's lemonade crate stuffed with seven-inch singles most of which were bought from Liverpool record shops.

But I did have another way to top up my vinyl habit.

My schoolmate, Stephen Coggins, had a mum who worked for a company that replenished jukeboxes and she would often leave me records without sleeves and sleeves without records. I would keep the Punk singles and lash the Boney M, Bonny Tyler, Wombles and Kenny Rogers ones. Punk sleeves without records were Sellotaped to my bedroom wall. A frieze of picture sleeves began to hide the woodchip. I was a Punk record sleeve Twitcher.

I became addicted to the jackets that wrapped around the music. I wanted to be a cut and paste version of a Saville Row tailor, armed with a scalpel, glue and paint.

Sex Pistols and Buzzcocks' sleeves became a sort of art gallery soap opera for me and I couldn't wait for the next episode to arrive and live in my lemonade crate next door to 'The Day The World Turned Dayglo', 'Love You More', 'Cost of Living' ep or 'Jimmy Jimmy'.

Thinking back, for me there were two art galleries in Liverpool - The Walker and Probe Records. I didn't know it at the time, but both provided me with a good education.

It's why I went to Art School...

CHARLIE HARPER

On finding a new watering hole, somewhere we could drink the night away, we discovered a great little bar in Covent Garden called Chagaramas. It was a lesbian club but our little gang was into Iggy, Dolls and the Velvets, and looked even more weird than the regulars and were never refused entry.

However, one night we arrived and things had changed, there were boys hanging around the entrance and a far buzzier crowd.

The club had changed its name too, it was now the Roxy and bands played almost every day when before just Friday night was band night. I was 30 and my band were in their early 20s and didn't go out after the pubs closed at 11pm. But one night I persuaded them to go, telling them that this was the future of rock 'n' roll.

Surprisingly, they were impressed and told me that they were going to dump the R&B and play Punk Rock. I told them that although I loved the music, I was just an old Rocker and we parted company.

The next week a friend came along and told of a guy he met at a party who played guitar and was looking for a band. His name was Nicky Garratt and on our first meeting we ended up writing half our song list, adding my few songs and one or two covers. The UK Subs were born.

In the Roxy, we only needed to play for 20 minutes but in bars we had to do two sets, sometimes dragging Greg Brown my flatmate down with his sax to play long solos to fill out the set for the first few rapturous weeks.

When the Roxy shut down, we played the farewell party which was recorded and did become the follow up to the Roxy album. We were lucky to be picked up on by John Peel who played our tracks on his BBC show. We got an independent record deal with our first single 'C.I.D.' which topped the Indie charts

The rest, as they say, is history… Love, Chas

CHRIS DIFFORD

1 August 1977, and I went to see Generation X, The Lurkers, Art Attacks and Steel Pulse at The Vortex club. Walking down the steps into the club, I felt out of place and intimidated. I had been before to see The Cortinas and Chelsea, who we shared an office with at the time, but it was still a big walk.

The Punk movement felt aggressive and reminded me of my skinhead days a few dark years before. Young drunk wannabes fell about all over the place looking for someone to bump into, shove or spit at. The best I could do was try and blend in, so I went to Boots and bought some safety pins. I attached them to my shirt and marched in with the leather jacket hanging open and the swagger. Billy Idol made a good job of winding everybody up and the place shook to the foundations. I liked Billy's attitude but not the songs or his pumped-up ego which he chucked around like a bad smell.

The room overheated and soon the crowd was swaying this way and that until I'd been levitated 50 feet or more without lifting a leg or moving a muscle. It was like being down the Valley at a Charlton game before the nice seats were cemented into place. I left for a Chinese meal, deaf and a little drunk. It was a bear-pit of a place and as much as I longed to be part of the scene, I think I preferred the cosy pub on my street corner.

Some weeks later, Generation X opened for Squeeze on home turf in Greenwich.

CLEM BURKE

The so called 'Punk scene' in NYC was somewhat different from what was happening in the UK. Dare I say, while London was more political/anarchistic, the NYC scene was more intellectual/arty. With our early success in Blondie we were able to see it from both sides. This, I think, enabled us to have a great overview of the whole scene and find inspiration; a muse in both the fans and the bands on both sides of the pond.

In NYC, CBGB was literally like Rock 'n' Roll high school or college for that matter. A lot of friendships were made that still endure to this day. Also at CB's, it was great to be able to see the groups that were coming over from the UK.

It was always great to hang in London with musician friends from back home. I recall a great night out with Joan Jett going to the Music Machine to see Vicious White Kids, a band with members Sid Vicious, Rat Scabies, Steve New and ironically Glen Matlock. I remember Marc Bolan was there hanging out with the rest of The Damned who were about to head out on tour opening for T Rex. I also have fond memories of running into Paul Weller at Dingwalls in Camden Lock.

In 1978, I was living in the Chelsea neighbourhood of NYC very near to the Chelsea Hotel. Nancy Spungen was a friend of ours and when she was murdered at the hotel things started to look very dark for a while. I couldn't believe this was happening around the corner from my apartment. Nancy, along with Sid, Jerry Nolan, Johnny Thunders, Joe Strummer and many others, didn't manage to make it out of the Punk scene alive but they all live on in my memory.

It really amazes me that after all this time there's still an interest in what went on in those few years of pop culture in the late seventies. It seems that it informs modern day pop culture to this day.

Long Live Punk!

DAVE PARSONS

The Conception...

The day the music changed, well it was a bit more than a day but it all happened relatively fast and was perfect timing for us. Even at this time, most of the gigs I went to still had that hippie feel about them – joss sticks burning, the long hairs smoking dope and everyone seated.

On the 4th of July, Jimmy and I headed up to London's Roundhouse, well known in those days as a bit of an old hippie hangout. We were there to see the first ever performance in this country by a New York band called The Ramones whose first album had been released a few months before earlier.

Jimmy had procured a copy and lent it to me which I'd taped to cassette. The concert took The Ramones by surprise as much as it did the audience. Outside of New York the band had only ever been met with a hostile response. It was this gig that changed everything for them, and of course their audience, of which we were a part. It was a full-on assault of the senses that lasted for about 35 minutes, barely a second's break between numbers. We were left dazed, high and begging for more. This approach left its mark on us. See, when promoters booked a band they would stipulate how long they would play and that was never going to work for us. We'd rather give everything we had in a short burst of energy, rarely lasting more than 45 minutes. For that, you got everything we had to give.

August 28th – Back at home late one evening, I turned the TV on to catch the end of Tony Wilson's programme *So It Goes* and was greeted by a shout of "Get off your arse" from this scrawny looking guy in a ripped up pink jacket, snarling into my living room.

I was pinned to my seat and felt like I'd been hit with a sledgehammer. What was going on? I'd never seen anything like this on the BBC before - welcome the Sex Pistols. It seemed like the Phoenix had finally risen!

The only band I'd seen prior to all this that hinted at something new was the Heavy Metal Kids.

It was first gig I'd been to where the audience actually felt scared - Gary Holton on stage with a syringe hanging out of his arm. Where all the old school were sitting with their feet up on the stage drinking beer, he swung a big chain from around his neck and neatly smashed all their glasses. I learnt a lot about attitude that night.

It was Friday 26 November 1976, and at the Walton playhouse Bobalouis/Excalibur are the first band on. We play a good set and get a good reaction from the audience, the band are all well happy with the night, but for me (especially after having just seen The Pistols) it felt like something was lacking. It all felt a bit safe, not enough edge. Next on was Sham 69. Jimmy walked on stage barefoot and wearing a torn shirt, Albie had the seat ripped out of his jeans with "Fuck you" written on his bum cheeks, I was blown away before they even played a note. The rest of the band weren't much cop and musically their set was lacking but they made up for with sheer energy and confidence, forcing a reaction – good and bad – from the unsuspecting audience.

The *Surrey Herald* wrote, "Punk Rock has gathered a cult following in London but perhaps Walton audiences are not yet prepared for this bizarre rock craze."

From this moment on, my friendship with Jimmy and Albie was set in stone. The three of us started hanging out together, to the exclusion of our other band members. We just seemed to think the same, have the same commitment to what we were doing and where we wanted to go, and I guess the same absolute belief in ourselves and the arena that Punk Rock was beginning to open up. It felt like we'd been born for this moment.

It wasn't long before we decided to form a new band. Several names were put up but nothing seemed to strike a chord. Because the name Sham 69 was Jimmy's and it hadn't been that long in existence, we decided to keep it.

I started to see how important chemistry was in making a successful band. I knew that no matter how good Bobalouis may have become, I didn't have the confidence that Jimmy had as a front man or his ability to open doors and move things forward. At the same time, Jimmy didn't have a writer in his old band with the same drive and ambition that I had, so together we became a viable force. When I asked Jimmy where he got the name from, he said, "It was after a football match in 1969 by our local football team Walton and Hersham, and someone had spray painted

Walton and Hersham 69 on the urinals at Hersham station. After a few months of people pissing on it, the Walton and Her had been erased, leaving just the sham 69 bit."

The musical tide of change was now definitely with us. The London orientated pub rock scene from places such as The Nashville Rooms, Red Cow, Croydon Greyhound and the Hope and Anchor, had been steadily setting the stage for Punk Rock, spawning such bands as Kilburn and the High Roads, Dr Feelgood, the great Graham Parker and the Rumour, Brinsley Schwarz etc. I remember turning on *Top Of The Pops* one night around this time, expecting the same old dross, but instead being blown away by a band called Eddie and the Hot Rods and their single 'Teenage Depression'.

While driving back from my brief but increasingly depressing Plessey Radar job one afternoon, The Jam's 'In the City' came on the radio. It sent a shiver up my spine. Suddenly, there were bands that were actually talking to me again,

For the first time in my life, I felt like I was in the right place at the right time.

DEBSEY WYKES

Late seventies Cambridge was awash with students and hippies but not many Punks. There was however one place you could run into them, a small shop in King Street called 'Remember Those Oldies' which was the first in the town to stock Punk records and fanzines. The owner was a local impresario called Lee Wood who also ran Raw Records, home to The Killjoys, The Gorillas and Cambridge's very own Punk band The Users featuring Rachel's brother Andrew on drums.

One Saturday in May '78, we received a phone call from Lee asking if we would play THAT NIGHT! at the Raw Records 1st anniversary show. We had only formed Dolly Mixture in February, going on to play our first gig that April at a friend's party and this – our fourth – was to be at The Corn Exchange, the town's prime music venue! We had seen most of the big Punk groups play there and so to go from being in the audience one week to playing on stage the next was just unbelievable.

Never having met any bands from outside Cambridge let alone play with them, it was a daunting experience turning up at the cavernous Corn Exchange for a sound check with just a bass and two drumsticks and having to ask if we could possibly borrow anyone else's gear. We received a fairly frosty reception and the only people who responded favourably were the Nipple Erectors who were more than happy to help. They looked amazing and seemed so cool that we couldn't believe that they were actually smiling and talking to us.

It was a wonderful night for us although Rachel had to go home and revise for her 'O' levels as soon as we came off stage. The Nipple Erectors were fantastic but I don't remember much about the other bands apart from the fact that they played far too long meaning that Kevin Rowland's band The Killjoys only had time for one song before the plug was pulled at midnight.

A couple of weeks later Hester ran into the school classroom clutching a copy of the NME with a review of the gig which stated that we were one of the weirdest things they'd ever seen!

DUNCAN REID

Out with the old and in with the new (before the old comes back in again!)…

For about five minutes The Roxy was the place to be.

It sold horrible cans of warm beer and rasta DJs played nothing but dub reggae and made money on the side offloading huge spliffs to white kids. But it was small, suited the early days of Punk and gave many bands an important stage to play on.

It was also the setting for a night which summed up for me the feeling that the new was emerging to blow away the old.

Before one of The Boys' gigs one night, the word went around that Jimmy Page and Robert Plant were coming down to check us out.

Halfway through our set, I noticed a bit of a kerfuffle with our drummer, Jack Black. An overweight, bearded bloke was on stage causing a nuisance. "Let me have a blow man. Come on,

let me have a blow," he said as he trespassed on our space. We carried on playing at 100 mph as Jack shouted, "Fuck off. The DJ's over there. Go and see him for blow."

We found out later the bearded guy was John Bonham. He was enjoying us so much he wanted to join in. Such was our youthful arrogance we really didn't care. Led Zeppelin were old news and we were the future, so no big deal. Just another step in the transition from dinosaurs to a new order.

I've often thought about it later though, especially after Bonham died and Led Zeppelin became legendary as the godfathers of heavy metal, with Bonham heralded as one of the greatest drummers of all time.

What would it have been like? We were fast. Could he have kept up? He didn't know the songs. Could he have busked it?

Now if it had been Keith Moon, we definitely would have kicked Jack off his stool!

ED BAZALGETTE

Easy... April 77, the first Clash LP. My mate bought it the day it came out and said you have to come round and listen. Side one track one 'Janie Jones'. Fast urgent drums, sharp guitar stabs, the vocals a volley of half formed words that shouted and spat at you from the speakers. Even now listening to it after all this time you can't keep still. For years we'd been hearing music that was growing more and more distant, that we had no connection with. This sounded like it was for us, something we could call our own.

The rest of the record flew at you too. What stood out alongside the energy and anger was how short the songs were. At least half of them barely reached the 2 minute mark – that was a revelation – play it fast, keep it lean, get it done. And it wasn't mindless noise - forget the DIY 'you don't need to be able to play' attitude. These songs were brilliantly written and played, these were class musicians who knew their chops. R&B, rock n roll and pop, it's all there. And reggae. In the middle of side 2 there's 'Police and Thieves', the breakneck pace eased off for six minutes as they pay homage to Junior Murvin's classic anthem. Still the same passion but a different tempo, and with that killer bass riff front and centre.

That song was my inspiration too, even I could pick out the notes and chords on that one. Within a few weeks me and my mate had left our band and started our own. 'Police and Thieves' was the first song we learned to play. Fortunately no recordings of our version survive...

NEW VIC BANS 'PUNK' VIBRATORS

EDDIE EDWARDS

WHAT PUNK MEANT TO ME.   258 words

This is hard to answer as in the early 70's I was a music nut. Going to gigs, running a mobile disco and driving every aspiring, ~~band~~ group in my part of North London. I was hoping that one would find success and I could go on, and ~~find~~ tour the world with them. Mostly I realised they wanted only to play local gigs and then just as a hobby. I started to learn the bass and got nowhere and spoke to my old friend, guitarist John Ellis about forming a band. He pointed out that Pat Collier was a great bass player and that I could play drums as I usually sat and played when setting up for the bands I was ~~roadie~~ for. I also knew Knox was free and a good songwriter and guitarist and so the Vibrators were born. The idea was to get back to the roots, lots of fast short exciting songs and back to the spirit of the greats of the 50's and 60's. You have to remember this was the era of Yes, ELP and 8 minutes of pretentious operatic songs by Queen. I'd had enough of that. We started playing in Feb '76 and by the time of the Punk Festival in the 100 club were headlining and packing in crowds. I liked the fact we were seen as Punk and am proud to have helped kickstart the whole thing. Nearly 41 years later I still believe in these exciting 3 min songs. That's what it is to me. EXCITING MUSIC

GAYE BLACK

(WHO DESIGNED THESE GREAT MONTAGES)

A colour xerox flyer for the Wayne County and Adverts gig at the Roxy, a photo of Johnny Rotten by Ray Stevenson, gig tickets and passes and Ramones autographs on a folded up flyer from 1977..

GAYE BLACK

Damned photo by Erica Echenberg, stickers on my suitcase that I took on tour in 1977, background gift wrap from 1977 and acrylic.

Press photo of Iggy Pop and Motorhead promo photo, Iggy's dog collar, my passes from the Iggy/Adverts 1977 tour, a lock knife, and my collection of guitar picks from The Damned, Pistols, Stranglers and all those bands from 1977. Background is acrylic and collage

GAYE BLACK

Featured in this piece are photos given to me in 1977, complete with dirty marks where I had Sellotaped them to the wall back then. Also a home made Iggy sticker given to me by a fan, a picture of a rat cut out of a newspaper, and the Avon sign, all from my bass. Iggy Pop's dog collar, a Ramones promotional baseball bat, Ramones lyrics written on an envelope, a gig ticket, a gig flyer, an Adverts sticker, photos of a Damned gig with me singing on 'Neat Neat Neat', and a page from my 1977 diary. The background is acrylic on paper.

GLEN MATLOCK

I've got a totally different story from most people involved in Punk. For me, Punk was 1975-'76. That's when all the seeds were sown, when all the donkey work was done, when most of *Never Mind The Bollocks* was written.

In very early '77 I realized it was never going to work with Rotten. The minute he got his face in the paper he totally changed. He became worse than Elton John – arrogant and conceited. When we first got together he was never a shrinking violet but we had a good working relationship and that's where all the songs came from.

The band went to Holland and we did two nights at the Paradiso in Amsterdam. In Rotterdam, we got bottled off stage. We also did Rock Circus and appeared with Golden Earring, Three Degrees and a dwarf who spun plates. I'd love to see some footage from that.

Anyway, that's when it all went tits up for me. When we got back to London, I had a meeting with Malcolm, Steve and Paul at Food for Thought in Covent Garden. At the meeting Paul said to me, "Can't you just pretend that you like John?" I was annoyed with Paul and Steve because I didn't think they were backing me up, especially as I'd put so much effort into the band. At that meeting, we agreed to go our separate ways. It was all perfectly amicable and we shook hands

I did find out that they'd already tried rehearsing with Sid behind my back which I thought was pretty shitty. About ten days later, Malcolm called me and said it wasn't working out with Sid and he wanted me to come back. I had a meeting with him in the Blue Posts, a pub behind the 100 Club, and Malcolm said he wanted me to "kick the doors down" and be the bass player. I told him he'd played me the wrong way and that it was too late.

A few days after that, the NME published a story about Malcolm sending them a telegram saying I'd been sacked because I liked The Beatles. He never said that to my face. Even to this day, 40 years later, people still say the same fucking thing to me. It's a stigma I can't shake off which is so galling because it was a pack of lies.

I didn't like the way it was all becoming Malcolm's media exercise, like a fucking cartoon strip. I just wanted to be in a band like The Who, by the kids for the kids. That's a cliché I know, but that's the way I saw it. All that stuff about being banned from playing was a crock of shit. Promoters would come up to me and say they'd love to put us on but when I told Malcolm he'd say no and I thought it was all dishonest.

To this day, Malcolm never realised that we were any good musically. He really believed that we were like a loud version of the Bay City Rollers. He didn't get the fact that people dug it because, in John's own words, we had "oodles of content." Our music struck a chord with people. And even though I had issues with John, he was one of the great rock performers.

And let's face it, if I hadn't have been in the band they wouldn't have had the first three singles.

So, I was watching the whole '77 thing unravel from a different perspective. As the year progressed and I saw what was happening with the Pistols, I thought, good for them – I was getting paid for them to promote the songs we wrote together. I also thought, fuck 'em. They'd said too much shitty stuff about me.

Mike Thorne, who was an A&R guy at EMI, rang

me up out of the blue and invited me out for a curry. He said EMI saw me as the main tunesmith in the band but knew there a problem. "If you don't resolve the situation we'd be interested in anything you come up with." I'd just turned 20 and was getting all this shit from everybody. I wondered if it was all more trouble than it was worth.

Then I thought, if EMI think that about me, what about the other record companies? So, while The Pistols were starting to do their thing, I was getting the Rich Kids together. It would've been very easy for me to form a band then and become a second division Sex Pistols, but I didn't want to do that. I wanted to do something different and that's why I teamed up with Midge Ure.

In 1975, Malcolm and Bernie Rhodes went on a trip around UK checking out old clothes for Malcolm's teddy boy shop. They went into a music shop in Glasgow trying to sell an amp and you can imagine, they stuck out like sore thumbs in that city in '75. There was a young guy in the shop and he stood out too because he had short hair. Everybody then, from the bank manager to the milkman, had long hair and flares.

When they came outside, the young guy was waiting for them and gave them his number. It was Midge. Around that time, we were looking for a singer. Wally Nightingale had been in the band then and Steve had been the singer. When Wally left, Steve moved to guitar. I called Midge from Malcolm's shop and spoke to his mum. "Hey, wee Jimmy," she shouted to him, "there's someone for you on the phone from London." I asked him if he was interested in joining the band because he had short hair. He said, "Thanks for asking but I'm doing this thing with a band called Slik and it looks like it's gonna go."

Anyway, while I was getting the Rich Kids together I must've tried out every singer in London. We were rehearsing in a place in Great Newport Street, where the Stones used to rehearse, and the bloke on vocals didn't have it. I remember walking round Leicester Square thinking what the fuck was I gonna do? I went into HMV and was flicking through the records

and came across the Slik album. They'd gone by then and I wondered what Midge was doing. I got in touch and he wasn't doing anything so he came down to London. I discovered he liked similar things to me musically and he had a great distinctive voice.

At the time, The Pistols were on the cover of *Investors Review* magazine and hailed as Businessmen of the Year and all I had were tax officers chasing me after me and I was living in a fucking squat in Stoke Newington. That's when I thought of the name – The Rich Kids. Plus, I'd been reading a lot of Cocteau's Les Enfants Terrible, "the children are so rich in thought." The name probably went over most people's heads at the time and probably wasn't that good in the first place. I just wanted to do the exact opposite of Punk, not because I hated it but anything that's successful is always different from what's going on around it. If the Pistols were doing stuff that was going around at the time, they'd have been a jazz funk band like Kokomo.

The very first time the Rich Kids played live was at the Hope & Anchor in '77. We were trying to blag our way into the pub to see The Police who were a four-piece then. The box office guy said the support band hadn't turned up and I said we'd play. He told us to pay the entrance fee of £1 each and if we were any good he'd give us our money back. We played four songs we'd rehearsed earlier and not only did he give us our money back but threw in a fiver on top!

When we left the Hope that night, we went to a party in a warehouse by the Thames and performed the songs again. The place was owned by the artist Anne Bean and she was wearing an apron that appeared to be made of boiled bacon. She looked like Lady Gaga and Midge couldn't believe it. The warehouse was on two levels and overlooked the river. Some bloke on the second level decided to piss over the balcony into the river but instead it went all over a couple directly below. The couple turned out to be Sid and Nancy, who were both completely out of it and I killed myself laughing.

I'd had a run in with Sid at the Roxy Club earlier

that year. Sid followed me into the toilet and said, "I'm the bass player now and you ain't. Bet you're choked." I told him I'd had enough of his mate (John was with him that night). I asked him if he could play and he said, 'Well…' I said I'd give him some lessons and he seemed quite pleased. I never did though.

I never saw the Pistols play once in '77.

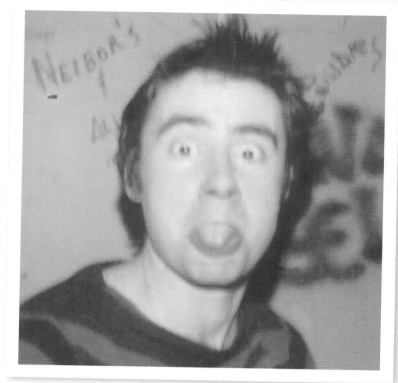

While I was doing the Rich Kids, Mick Ronson contacted me and ended up producing our debut album. Steve New was our guitarist. He was so young that we had to get his dad to sign release papers. First time I met him, Steve turned up with this art teacher who he was shagging at the time. After that first (and only) album, things started to go wrong. There'd been an NME-led backlash against the band. The mag carried a feature along the lines of 'Anarchy in the UK and Apathy in Birmingham'. We were being judged against the Pistols and it wasn't supposed to be anything like that. The Rich Kids were a different thing entirely. We were the Great White Hope at the beginning of '78 but I was getting coated by Rotten all the time in the papers and ended up drinking too much.

I was proud of the Rich Kids. We were like a bridge between Punk and New Romantic and probably a little bit ahead of our time – I would say that. When we played Barbarellas in Birmingham, Duran Duran were up front. And when we did a reunion show in London last year, Gary Kemp stood in for Steve New, God rest his soul. Gary said he was a big fan of the band.

The Kids lasted for about two years before Midge and drummer Rusty Egan wanted to become New Romantics and Steve and I wanted to rock out. Then, after the split, I was invited by Iggy Pop to play on his New Values tour in 1979.

Iggy came to the Lyceum to see the Rich Kids when Ian McLagan and Mick Ronson decided to play with us. It was an amazing evening – Steve Marriot turned up because he was trying to get the Small Faces back together and thought I was nicking his keyboardist and Steve Jones and Paul Cook showed and all of them were in the khazi arguing about who's had the most toot before we were due to play. I had to ask the DJ, Nicky Horne, to make an announcement – "Would

' God Save The Queen.
e on the new album and it may not be
for very long.
while you can.
s' God Save The Queen.
only as a single from Saturday May 28th
with the sign.

he's still known as the singer from The Jam. I was the bassist and that's the problem. If the singer in a band is good and he knows it, he can get another band. I've done some writing with Mick Jones and he said, "This is all good, Glen. The only problem is, you're not my Joe Strummer and I'm not your Johnny Rotten."

Punk was a sea change that hailed the end of the age of deference. It stirred things up. If I go to South America or Italy I invariably get some bloke from the local communist party come up to me and treat me as some kind of saviour; Che Guevara with knobs on. Steve says in his book that we simply made records and what people chose to think about it was up to them. Mind you, John thought he was the saviour.

What you can't take away from the Pistols is that we all met early on through Malcolm's shop which was the antithesis of what was going on in London at that time on a Saturday afternoon. It was next door to Granny Takes A Trip where the Stones and The Faces got their clothes. We were 17 years-old and there'd be Bryan Ferry and Anthony Price strolling down the Kings Road. Malcolm thought they were tossers and so we did too. They were all multi- millionaires and we didn't have a pot to piss in and Malcolm instilled in us a really good attitude. Steve was the biggest oik ever, like something out of a Jean Genet book, and so was Paul. And then we found John who, to me, was like Jonathan Swift. The only thing is, Swift didn't do butter adverts.

everyone please come out of the toilet coz you're due on stage!"

My time with the Rich Kids was more satisfying than the Pistols because I was calling the shots more. In every band there's a fall guy and I was the one in the Pistols and I didn't like it especially as I came up with a lot of the music and some of the lyrics. I wrote 'Pretty Vacant' – all of it. John changed two lines later. But the way the band performed those songs was great.

It's such a weird thing when I hear those records. I think I've written equally good songs but everything's measured against those. It's frustrating – I'd much rather live in the present and be judged on what I'm doing now knowing it's had a fair listening. Paul Weller does well but

I'm proud of my involvement in Punk. But I'm prouder still of all those people that used to come into the shop and went on to achieve so much in the fields of music, fashion, the arts, photography. The Pistols were a good year before everyone else. I remember talking to John when Caroline Coon and Jonh Ingham did tandem articles in their respective papers, *Melody Maker* and *Sounds*. I said to John I wasn't sure I got the gist of all this and he said, "I do. It says we were the first." I thought that went without saying but you have to ram things down people's throats.

I still see Paul, I've seen Steve but I haven't seen John since we walked off stage in Spain in 2008. That suits me fine...

HAZEL O'CONNOR

I wasn't around at the beginning of Punk as I was away dancing in Japan and then Beirut with a Cabaret troupe, but when I arrived back in the UK my brother Neil and his mates had formed a band called The Flys and made their own five-track ep with the main song being 'Love And A Molotov Cocktail'. Because of this, EMI signed them to a record deal and they went out on tour supporting The Buzzcocks.

I went to one of their gigs and was totally blown away by the energy of the songs by both The Flys and The Buzzcocks and I was bitten by the bug.

I went to see bands all the time at the 100 Club, the Rock Garden and the Marquee but the most memorable was seeing the Sex Pistols at Brunel University. What I loved about the Punk and new wave movement for me as a woman was that there was no judgement about being pretty or sexy as girl singers in the past had been regarded. We seemed judged by energy instead which appealed to me completely.

The lovely Poly Styrene and Siouxsie Sue and Pauline Murray from Penetration (who had the greatest voice) were my heroines and an inspiration so I asked my brother Neil how to get a record deal, naive as I was because it sounded like something you bought in a shop. He said you gotta write songs and do gigs and showed me how to construct songs.

The Flys performed on my early demos and I did my first gigs with the likes of Jim Toomey on drums, who was also in The Tourists, and Gary Tibbs on bass also of The Vibrators and later Roxy Music and Adam and the Ants. I supported bands like The Ruts for a fiver and loved the energy and diversity of it all.

I was described in the first review I got as a cross between Debbie Harry and Barbara Windsor of the new wave!

The best thing about Punk for me was you didn't have to be a copy of anyone else. It celebrated uniqueness as it kicked out the old fuddy duddy overblown music of the late sixties and early seventies and replaced it with a street, grass roots movement with an energy and garishness that shocked which was good as it was a reaction to the dreadful right wing government the UK was enduring and the dismantling of the steel and coal industries and the bashing of the unions and the working class. Youth was reacting and that was my Punk experience!!!! Something that the powers that be couldn't control.

Of course, they eventually bought into it and the wild animal was tamed by record deals and money…

the stranglers
NEW SINGLE

HUGH CORNWELL

'77,'77, all good Punks will end up in heaven...

It was the year when the system realised they'd left the gate open.

During '75 and '76 the interesting stuff had happened: various musically frustrated individuals had found each other in chaotic ways and bands had been formed. They stumbled through the hoops, learning how to play, how to perform, and, if they were lucky, how to write songs. There wasn't a gig circuit, just a word of mouth grapevine which kicked in when one of the bands managed to get a spot somewhere. We were more fortunate than some, as our managers controlled a few venues, so we were already on the ladder.

One of our most bizarre regular gigs was The Speakeasy, in Margaret Street, the late-night hangout for the musical elite, and impossible to get into unless you were playing there. Our ice-cream van would roll up outside and members of The Damned, Pistols, Clash, even Elvis Costello, would jump out of the back door carrying one of our guitars or a cymbal stand. Posing as one of our roadies got them into the club, where our heroes were binging the night away. The music establishment had been caught napping, and before they knew it a whole alternative system had been papier-mached together. So, when 1977 arrived we were all signed up and on to the next step. Several journalists had cottoned on earlier, and looked on bemused as the rest of the press, and the rest of the country, caught up and tried to digest what had happened.

IGGY POP

(From a 1978 interview by Barry Cain)

After every gig I need to get away. It's a psychological trick. I use the simplicity of distance, in miles, to enable me to gain a perspective of where I've just been. Then I can sit back and evaluate in a totally clinical way. This is a real dirty business a filthy business. I hate it. It's a big industry built on precarious foundations. So I try and keep myself apart from it as much as I can. I give everything I've got on stage and steer clear of the industry after that.

I'm afraid I'm a member of that terribly unfashionable school which adheres to the rule of giving people entertainment. My life revolves around my work. I'm not a very interesting international playboy.

Things I read about Bowie and me bear so little resemblance to what actually goes on. It's so predictable. I value everything we've done together. And there are things between us that will come to light in time. Projects we're working on now are years ahead of this era.

I seem to have found myself in a position to always be ahead of the next man. Everything I do is interpreted later. That why there's so much press about me. People are unable to understand what I'm at so all they become interested in are my attendant features – like vomiting a lot.

I'm often regarded as a boil, y'know, a big boil that has to be lanced.

Sure, I capitalise on the outrageousness. Instead of ignoring it I embrace it, accept it, and it brings me more fame and fortune. And the more fame and fortune I get, the more it enables me to play my music

And my music is like a high-pitched dog whistle. You either hear it or not. To me it's soothing. I need volume to drown out the rest of existence. It has this soporific effect, weakening almost, on me. But at the same time its sheer buoyancy keeps me afloat.

I get very scared about death but I guess I wouldn't mind dying on stage. It's bound to happen anyway. There are a lot of guys out there that hate me. One of them is gonna get up one night and BANG! shoot the fuck outta me.

My parents are pretty important to me. They have a great deal to do with whatever position I've attained now. They're the best. A lot of guys in rock don't talk much about their folks. That's 'cos they're now fighting the battles they should have fought when they were seven. Y'know, they say now, "Hey Mum. I don't wanna eat my eggyweggy," when they should have said it years ago. Me, I always told my mum if I didn't want my eggyweggy. Sure my parents are shocked by some of my actions. They always wanted me to be reasonably in one piece. Still, better shocked by me than strangers, eh?

I have a son, Eric, who lives in California at the moment and rides horses all day. I don't see much of him. I provide for him but that's all. I guess looking after him financially is my way of doing something worthwhile.

'I don't see much of his mum either. That's the way I like it. I move around a lot. Don't like the same surroundings.

I once described myself as 'King of the Failures'. That's apropos. I'd just been reading Cocteau when I said that. See, all the successes I know are really boring little cheeses. Once those guys are exposed to that dirty thing called the public they become ignorant and inhuman.

I don't like to disappoint my fans. I'm their superman and before I walk out on stage I look at myself in the mirror and think, "Wow, Iggy, you're pretty good looking."

You know something? I think I'm the greatest...

JEAN-JACQUES BURNEL

I have a problem with this whole period. You see, I felt very much part of it.

After all we were the ones who played with Patti Smith.

We were the ones who played with the Ramones.

We were the ones who played in the provinces and got attacked every night.

Yet the poseurs in London got the front covers.

We actually outsold The Clash, the Sex Pistols, The Damned, who all came to our gigs before they had formed, yet we were the ones who got called bandwagon jumpers and got ostracised by those who had previously been friendly to us.

Their time came and went.

Now, The Stranglers are selling out everywhere.

More and more people have got the courage to acknowledge our contribution to the period and yet self-appointed 'experts' on it like Jon Savage and by default, the BBC, have written us out of history.

So, bollocks to it I say.

JOE STRUMMER

(from a 1977 interview by Barry Cain)

Bombsite Soliloquy

The fact that 'White Riot' has jumped so much is good – but it's not good enough. I want more. I want a number one. It's not getting any radio plays because the people in control of the airwaves are so fucking against us. They want to stamp us out. They feel threatened. They are Nazis. We ain't, but we want to persecute, to fucking wipe them off the face of the earth.

I've found you can only really think when you're completely alone. It's impossible when other people are around. That's why I only live late at night because that's when I can do strange things. A lot of the time I get molested by the police because they want to know what I'm up to. It's dark and getting darker.

I foresee restrictions, not just for individuals but for entire governments, cities, nations. I foresee the return of conscription. I foresee less personal freedom and the introduction of identity cards. I see numbers.

I can feel it.

The government wants ultimate control and if they don't get it they lose. So, it stands to reason they're going to do everything in their fucking power to obtain that control. But I don't think that's frightening. If I did, I couldn't live. I know I'm never gonna be able to beat them so I don't believe in other people. Other people are fucking morons – they must be to stand for all this.

And when the government gets ultimate control, all I can see are bombsites and a handful of survivors. Roll the credits – end. You'll soon know when that control comes – things will start booming. Industry will thrive, unemployment will come down, people will march through the streets waving banners proclaiming their willingness to die for Queen and country. And I'll get my head kicked in.

The Clash can't change people – we can only create an atmosphere. If people want to change they will. I have a great time banging guitars and shouting. People can read too much into that and it makes me sick. They're stupid creeps. All this talking about how people can gain from what we do makes me puke.

Lawrence of Arabia was my only hero 'cos I thought it was real smooth him just coming out of England and leading the Arabs.

I find myself in a void, and it's a good void. I've always known what to do and always known what I'm doing it for. I'm smart. I'm lucky and luck is a dominant factor in life. You make your own luck by grabbing opportunities, and I grab opportunities by following the Cherokee Indian way. When they have to make a decision, they always choose the most reckless course of action. I always like to have my hands on the steering-wheel.

I suppose I'm like this because people have walked all over me in the past. When they do that I'm interested. I want to know why so they won't do it again. When I was nine I went to a boarding-school. On the first day I was surrounded by a bunch of boys who frogmarched me to the bathroom where I was confronted by a bath full of used toilet paper, a smear of shit on each sheet. They said I had to get in. If I refused they'd beat me up.

I got beaten up.

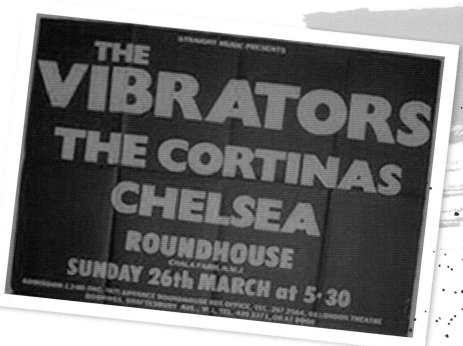

JOHN ELLIS

By the middle of 1977, The Vibrators had been touring extensively for some time and had released one album and several singles. Now it was time to get down to writing the next album, so we made a group decision to relocate to Berlin for a few months.

Why that wonderful walled city? We'd played there several times and were beginning to build up a local following. At that time, it was an edgy place but the atmosphere was charged with creativity. Our German promoter, Moishe Moser, had become a good friend by then and, because he was an artist in his own right, he seemed to know a lot of very interesting Berliners. And Bowie had chosen to record there, too.

So off we went to a little flat close to the wall that our promoter had rented for six months. We got down to writing, partying and doing occasional gigs. At that time, the Red Army Faction (RAF), also known as the Baader-Meinhof Gang, were creating havoc across Germany and the polizei were desperate to catch them. On 5 September 1977, the RAF kidnapped a major German industrialist called Hanns Martin Schleyer. They wanted to use him as a bargaining chip to force the release of the gang's leaders from prison in Stuttgart. The prisoners included Andreas Baader and Gudrun Ensslin.

The police had asked the public to be vigilant and watch out for unusual activity. Some of the press had suggested the IRA were helping the gang. On the 18th of October, after learning that Baader, Ensslin and two others had been found dead in prison, the kidnappers killed Schleyer and left his body in the boot of a car.

A few days before, our promoter had suggested we spend a weekend in a farmhouse he was renting in the countryside, so we happily left the city for a few days. During the third night, I was woken with a painful prodding in my chest and the sound of very loud German voices. As I slowly opened my eyes, I realised I was looking down the barrel of an automatic rifle. And at the end of it there was a very pissed off German soldier. When I got up I could see Knox, Eddie and Gary were getting the same treatment. We were marched out of the farmhouse into the cold night where we found our promoter explaining the reason for us being there. There were soldiers and police everywhere, many with dogs and there were several helicopters overhead. Moishe assured us we would be OK.

Apparently, a diligent neighbour had seen our van with English number plates arrive that afternoon. They thought we might be the IRA and called the cops. So, one of us made a call to our record label contact who was able to confirm our story, albeit in the middle of the night. For the rest of our stay there always seemed to be a helicopter overhead and on subsequent visits to Germany, I was always pulled out of the passport queue for more questions.

So, there you are. Just another day in the life of your average rock 'n' roll band in that glorious year of 1977.

JENNIE BELLESTAR

I was introduced to Punk by my wanna-be closet DJ boyfriend Steve who was working at a record shop and bringing home the latest stock. We got to sample all the pre- and new releases. This included Sex Pistols, Clash, Stranglers, Blondie, Per Ubu, Mink Deville, Jonathan Richman & The Modern Lovers, 999, Damned, Jam, Devo, the list is endless.

Most of these artists we saw live, many at The Roundhouse in London. But one night sticks out the most and that was in 1978 where things were a bit hazy for me. I was living with Steve and our housemates who were delightfully irresponsible and decadently debauched most of the time. We'd regularly saunter into the West End but one night we decided to go and see Jonathan Richman & The Modern Lovers at the Hammersmith Odeon.

I had a green afro, tight ripped T shirt and a pair of jeans so tight that if I was a fella I would be hitting all the high notes. Those jeans looked like they were painted on and were held together by

at least ten safety pins; not good if one is dying for a pee, I can tell ya.

After the gig had ended, the place was awash with Punks and new wave fans sporting every colour you can imagine in the hair department. We thought we looked pretty cool at the time but there were a bunch of people that took offence to our look and they had been lying in wait across the road getting ready for us to leave the venue. They were Hammersmith's very own teddy boys looking like they had time travelled from the fifties into the seventies. I heard someone shout, "Run for it!" and the next thing, we were running for our lives down the street. I was jumping over barriers and running into buildings being chased by hundreds of them and they were there to damage us. Later, one of our flat mates came back sporting a black eye and all sorts.

Other memories of that era were hanging out down the Kings Road and getting the latest stuff from BOY and Vivienne Westwood's Shop SEX.

JOHN LYDON

*(from a 2007 interview
by Barry Cain)*

I only knew we were doing the Grundy interview on the day. It's very important you understand that. I also didn't get a lift home after because Malcolm panicked so much he shot off immediately in the limo and I had to go home on the tube on my own. Nothing on earth looked like me and if I was on my own, I was a target.

There was plenty of sham in the Pistols and that was the shame of it. But most of the sham was coming from the management side because Malcolm didn't have a contributing role really, so he had to invent an image for himself as master manipulator. That suited his purpose no end. But Malcolm became a confused, dithering old twit.

'It's a shame I never got on with Malcolm but he never gave me the chance. I suppose I was too far ahead of the game for him. He could manipulate Steve, Paul and Glen because they were impressed by the shock and the T-shirts with 'Cambridge Rapist' on them but to me that was twot, silly stuff, childish but good fun. I hit bigger issues right from the start. We could be similar, we're both Aquarius. Look, Malcolm was clever and I enjoyed parts of his company very much but I never enjoyed the resentment and laziness.

I like life. Even when I go into dismal mode it's still a form of celebration. In 1977 all these bastards were trying to put me down again. I don't blame anyone and anything other than my own insecurities but I managed it and I enjoyed it and I thrived on it. Whenever I walked anywhere it was war – I've still got the scars to show for it. When I got attacked in Highbury in 1977 that was West Ham. Got them, though, got them lovely. What do you fucking think? Do you think we ran around bragging in the newspapers when we got them back?

In '77 I never saw in British society any room made for intelligence. It was always privilege over intelligence. It goes way back and I've never seen any good results from posh, rich bastards; not ever, not in the history of mankind. I've got great-grandfathers and uncles who fought in two world wars and the injuries they suffered were appalling – one of them had his anus blown out, for Chrissake. I was brought up witnessing this travesty, this mutilation of human beings. I knew I was raised simply to be cannon fodder for the next bunch of political geniuses that would get us involved in yet another idiotic war. Look, if you're not greedy it's a good start. Making money shouldn't be a motivation. It ain't the answer.

I know I'm belligerent, I can't help it. I make mistakes, I make enemies when I shouldn't. I don't mean to but I do because of, ha ha, the Mouth. The Mouth from the South. I suppose that's a direct result of the old Sex Pistols gigs up north when there wouldn't be a single night without 20 or 40 lads lined up to kick our fucking brains in. And in the middle of all that Malcolm booked us in Barnsley, Bolton, Bradford, all the fucking Bs up there, including a teddy-boy convention starring the Sex Pistols. Every teddy boy in the north of England turned up to kill us. But guess what? They didn't because they liked us.

Scarborough was another one where we had 200 lads who wanted to kill us. I said, "All right, I'm all alone on this big empty stage and there you are but I've got a mike stand." And I held it up in a threatening way and it did the trick. So I got cocky with that stand over the months – that's how I lost my front teeth. I got used to holding on to the mike stand offstage and I was at the Screen on the Green when a girl accidentally pushed the bottom of the stand as it was in my hands and it hit me in the mouth and I lost my two front teeth. We had a gig the next night and you didn't cancel gigs then, not like now, especially with American Punk bands like the Marilyn Mansons, 'Ooh, I've hurt me ankle – cancel the tour.' It was a holiday weekend and Malcolm said we didn't have the money to pay for an emergency dentist so I had to break into a local off-licence and nick a bottle of brandy to keep myself pissed to dull the pain.

I don't think I'm a dumb man. I never have, right? I've had a lot of mental problems in my life as a result of meningitis but I've overcome them and I've never been a parasite on the system. That in itself is my own self-achievement, that and

Rotten!

SEX PISTOLS

"Look, I want to change the music business right? I want to change all that . . . But it'll take years. I'll have to do it more skilfully this time. But it'll be with a vengeance. And they won't know."

making the word 'bollocks' legal, something you could wear on the beach in a fashionable little number. Did you know I went to the court case in Nottingham and Malcolm didn't turn up because he thought we were gonna lose and there might be a problem? This is why when he ran for mayor he didn't really run for mayor. He was never about commitment. He didn't follow things through. He always wanted other people to do it for him. But that's what I call an artist. You must understand 'The Rabbit Song' is about such people.

One of the worst periods of my life was when me and Jah Wobble lived in Edmonton just after the demise of the Pistols. He was a Tottenham lad and we rowed all the time. The house we lived in only cost six quid a week because it was supposed to be haunted. It fucking was too – by us! Strummer came over one night. He was all right. I didn't hate him. He was a pub-band bloke. He was older and had this ridiculous Cockney accent that wasn't quite right. He used to really drive me crazy. What the hell are you talking about Joe? This is why Joe Strummer ended up in a house in the country as a lord. He did everything wrong. Do you understand? Joe became the landed gentry and that was irrefutably wrong. It's nice to earn it but it's not nice to buy it. Beyond that little world or schism it was really ridiculous because there'd be Joe Strummer running around with all the posh towels, the steel towel-rail people. It was awful trying to get past their middle-class

sensibilities. We'd still be banned in clubs where the likes of Joe were accepted because he had, what, ambassador credentials?

Anyway, Joe came over to see the place, which had been bombed in the war and a woman died in the bathroom. When I took a shower – the first time in my life I'd ever had one and I'm still wary of them, I'm primitive – the soap would move backwards and forwards in its dish Wobble got really frightened after seeing something run down the stairs. He thought it was me until he realised I was in the kitchen all the time. There were a couple of hard-core hooligan mates staying with us that night and we all slept in one room because we were shitting ourselves. And the door would swing open and close all night and we were all shaking. One of the blokes was convinced it was my reggae records that were responsible for it all – 'We mustn't be tempting the demons with that mad dark shit.'

Was it mass psychosis and weakness in us or was it the drugs? We refused to pay the rent – we had no money – and the landlord turned up with all these thug guys. We invited them in but they refused because they'd heard about the ghosts. We thought this was wonderful, we're haunted and it's rent-free!

We later realised they were more likely scared of us.

NEVER MIND THE BANS

Dear Madam,

The Sex Pistols

Thank you for your letter of the 17th November regarding the proposed visit of the above band to the Cambridge Corn Exchange. This has now been discussed and it has been decided, regretfully, that we will not be able to offer the use of the Corn Exchange for their proposed concert.

Yours faithfully,

City Amenities and Recreation Officer

CITY OF CAMBRIDGE
Amenities and Recreation Department
Kett House
Station Road

GLC
New address w.e.f. 12 Dec. 1977
Room 654
The County Hall, SE1 7PB
Telephone direct—01-633
For general enquiries dial—
01-633 6000

Greater London Council
Parks Department

Chief Officer
James C. Kennedy

233 High Holborn London WC1V 7DN

of the 1978 tour has been an opportunity to witness a concert obtain at Alexandra Palace, I find it diffi to 6000 at a venue without permanently fixed seating such as the Great Ha not create management difficulties. Possible disturbance to residents in the immediate locality is also a factor which concerns me besides to users of other parts of the Palace building.

In all the circumstances, I, as licensee of Alexandra Palace, am not prepared to seek a licence to allow the proposed concerts.

Yours sincerely,

James C. Kennedy.

UGH OF WOLDS

Drive, Bridlington
Telephone Bridlington (0262) 78255
/PMX/1 When calling please ask for: Mr. Clifton
ATTENTION OF MRS. PURDENCE 2nd November 1977

. Purdence,

THE SEX PISTOLS

refer to your letter dated 24th October 1977 ur subsequent telephone call with Mr. Clifton ing the above.

I have now heard from my Chairman and Vice man on the proposed dates, and regret to inform that they will NOT give the Council's consent to booking. Please, therefore, cancel all provisional ings made.

Apologies for any inconvenience caused.

Yours sincerely,

B. A. Myford
Director of Tourism and
Resort Activities.

Cowbell Agency Ltd.,
153, George Street,
LONDON W1H 5LB.

BELLE VUE (MANCHESTER)
HYDE ROAD MANCHESTER M12 5PT 061-223 1331

Dear Mrs. Prudence,

Thank you for your letter 23rd November. I passed on all the relevant information to our Divisional Director, who yet again presented our case to the main Board in London, but unfortunately he met with a totally negative response. Therefore I regret to inform you that there is no chance at all of Belle Vue hosting the Sex Pistols for their forthcoming tour.

Please accept my personal apologies for putting you to the trouble of furnishing me with references, but I did sincerely feel that this might help the decision. However, the adverse publicity combined with the notorious reputation of this particular group have proved to be an insurmountable barrier.

However, may I wish you a successful tour with this band in the new year, and wish everyone at Cowbell and yourself a very Happy Christmas and prosperous 1978.

Yours sincerely,

D. JOHN HAMPSON.
Controller.

MARCH TOUR 78

RANK LEISURE SERVICES
439-445 Godstone Road Whyteleafe Surrey CR3 0YG
Telephone: Upper Warlingham (STD Code 08832) 3355
Telex: 262305 Cable Rankorg Whyteleafe Surrey

ENTERTAINMENT & CATERING DIVISION
26 October, 1977

THE SEX PISTOLS

As I have tried to explain to promoter after promoter, agent after agent, there is no way in which the Rank Organisation will become involved with the Sex Pistols.

My own personal opinion does not even come into consideration when the Board have stated quite clearly that we are not to allow the Band to play in any of our venues.

As you are aware, our attitude to New Wave and Punk is extremely liberal and many bands play our venues, but it is the opinion of our Senior Executive that due, as you say to the unfortunate reputation of the Sex Pistols that it is not in the best interest for our company to become associated with them.

I have taken note of your final paragraph and thank you for it and I can assure you that the matter is constantly being put before our senior people for re-assessment of the situation, but as you are aware, the words 'Sex Pistols' are rather emotive words, but I must say that Rank as a company are playing more Punk/New Wave than any other major company.

I am sorry to be so negative, I hope you will be able to understand our point of view.

Yours sincerely,

S.J. Tegg
Promotions and Publicity Manager

Directors: Rank Leisure Services Limited Registered in London under No 455220
Chairman T E Chilton
R J Dulfield (Managing Director)
L Small (Assistant Managing Director)
J W Davies Shiva King G Pinches
Registered Office 11 Hill Street London W1X 8AE England

CITY
DERBY BOROUGH COUNCIL
BATHS AND ENTERTAINMENTS DEPARTMENT

Chief Baths & Entertainments Officer.

Yours sincerely,

N. G. Robb.

Ref: The Sex Pistols

Further to your letter regarding the possible visit of the Sex Pistols to Derby, after consultation with the Chairman of the Leisure Committee we feel that it would be inadvisable at the present time in view of the unfortunate publicity the band received in December last year. I am aware the media surrounded them then.

We, therefore, regret that at the present time we cannot make our halls available. I should however, be pleased to discuss with you the possibility of other concerts if you so desire.

Bath City Council

Dear Mr Jackson

: THE SEX PISTOLS

ank you for your letter of 10 November, and I am sorry have not replied to you before.

egret that I am unable to accede to your request to the Pavilion next year for two concerts in connection the above group.

unfortunate reputation they have gained seems to bring s wake inevitable scenes of violence and resulting , and I do not feel inclined to subject the City's uitable hall or its staff to this possibility. If, r, your tour next year creates more favourable stances, I would of course be extremely happy to der this decision.

ou for considering Bath and I hope your tours next l be stimulating and peaceful.

cerely

Leisure services

SEX WILL PISTOLS PLAY

DECEMBER TOUR 77

Tickets: £1.75
If you are charged more DEMAND a refund

JORDAN MOONEY

I know this is about 1977 but a bit of '75 has to be included for me mainly because it painted such a vivid picture amongst the grey and beige backdrop of Britain at that time.

430 Kings Road had gained much notoriety which led the police to our door and hence the confiscation of what was deemed by the old bill, the fuzz, the wooden tops, as being openly obscene. Malcolm and Vivienne were charged under the 1864 obscene exhibition act of displaying items in the window, more specifically, the naked cowboys' T shirt. This in their view was likely to corrupt the general public and in particular minors.

Now of course, we all know for certain that when you try to enforce these draconian values on young people they will rebel even more. Much like the Sex Pistols never being allowed to be at the number one spot in the charts.

After the T shirt episode, we continued to window display as normal with one eye out for the Sweeney and always ready to remove the offending items at the drop of a helmet. Our main stock was kept in the toilet upstairs so that if we were raided again not all of it would be taken. When the New York Dolls came to the shop they were very impressed with the whole image, both of the shop and us.

For anyone who hadn't experienced it, it's hard to imagine the mixture of styles there. Rubber and leather fetish wear mixed with the raw and powerful graphics that adorned the shirts. These acts of rebellion all led up to 1977 and painted that year with very different colours, colours you could mix and make your own works of art in your clothes, attitude and music.

I felt truly at home in this environment as I'd been expressing myself like this since I was a child. It also helped to construct a gateway for me to walk through and enabled me to act in the film 'Jubilee', manage and sing with Adam and the Ants, play some part in the success of the Sex Pistols, enjoy first hand *Never Mind The Bollocks*, contribute to The Pistols first TV appearance, experience the tremendous Ramones concerts that were so full of energy and refusing to leave the boat when the police boarded it during the Sex Pistols Jubilee party.

All this was played out against the damp squib that was Queen's Jubilee celebrations.

This is not nostalgia but history.

SO YOU

QUICKIE QUIZ!

This is the quiz to sort out the skunks from the punks. If you think you're a punk you may be in for a shock! Our quiz will sort you out . . .

1. You've just bought a new eye make-up kit to experiment with. Do you:
a) Try 'n' create that natural look.
b) Match up the shadow with your outfit.
c) Draw a ring shape from your eye to your eyebrow and fill it in with bold black and white stripes.

2. Your mum gives you a large black polythene bag she thinks you'll find useful. Do you:
a) Use it to store odds and ends.
b) Cut holes for your head and arms and wear it as a dress.
c) Put it under your bed and forget about it.

3. You've got to a party and there are 3 unattached boys. Which one do you go for:
a) The smart one in the sports jacket with the E-type jag parked outside.
b) The one who looks strange but interesting.
c) The scruff in the corner with the safety pin in his ear who keeps flicking crisps at everyone.

4. You're at a dance but nobody seems to be dancing. Do you:
a) Stand at the side looking

pretty, hoping somebody will notice you.
b) Hide in the ladies loo for a while.
c) Get up on the floor by yourself and start gyrating like a road drill.

5. You decide it's time to get yourself some new jewellery. Do you:
a) Get yourself a set of matching pearls that complement your new twinset.
b) Get some metal chains from your local department store.
c) Save up for some real diamonds.

6. Your idea of a great night out is:
a) Sitting at your local rubbish tip with a few mates and swearing about other people's refuse.
b) A candle-lit dinner with your boyfriend, gazing dreamily into your jellied eels.
c) Going to bingo with your mum.

7. You get an unexpected present of a few pounds. Do you:
a) Open up an account with a building society.
b) Get on down to your local record shop and get stuck into JAM!
c) Buy some fancy frilly underwear.

8. You are at the bus stop and two women start staring and pointing at your short skirt and fish-net tights. Do you:
a) Walk down the road to the next bus stop.
b) Feel embarrassed but try to pretend you hadn't noticed.
c) Hitch your skirt up even further and tell them to get lost.

THUNK YOU'RE A PUNK?!

YOUR PUNK SCORE!

1. a 0, b 5, c10.   5. a 5, b10, c 0.
2. a 0, b10, c 5.   6. a10, b 5, c 0.
3. a 0, b 5, c10.   7. a 0, b10, c 5.
4. a 5, b 0, c10.   8. a 5, b 0, c10.

(TO FIND OUT WHAT YOUR SCORE MEANS TURN TO PAGE 30!)

JOHNNY THUNDERS

*(from a 1977 interview
by Barry Cain)*

When we started to play rock'n'roll it was a way of life. You can't play it legitimately if you're Black Sabbath. Even the Stones don't play legit. They used to until Ron Wood joined. Now they got no roots. And the new bands are too political. We ain't political at all. The only politics we wanna sell is the changing of the drug laws.

You know what? If you were arrested in New York for being drunk, like you are here, there would be a lot of cops with broken heads. You should hear the news there – "This guy got killed, this guy got murdered, this guy got tortured."

There are more clowns than good guys in music. British bands don't play as well as American bands. Rock'n'roll is simply an attitude – you don't have to play the greatest guitar. It makes me laugh when people acclaim our musicianship and technical brilliance. The Dolls proved you don't need to be technically far ahead of anyone else to be accepted. We know our five chords.

I was once gonna play in a band with Iggy Pop and y'know something, David Bowie's like a sponge soaking everything up that he hears. I wouldn't let him near me with a ten-foot pole. He's just an old English beatnik. Iggy never asked him into his world – Bowie dragged him into his.

I've finally decided I wanna change our name to the Junkies because it shows we're a no holds-barred band. I don't like 'The Heartbreakers'. I wanna sell more than music. I wanna sell art. Rock'n'roll is cheap. We've hit the Punks, the kids who've seen it all.

All the new bands think they're gonna change the fucking world – but all they're gonna change is their nappies. Johnny Rotten is Dr Jekyll and Mr Hyde. He tries too hard to live up to his image and he comes across like a pussycat. On his own, he's a nice guy. Steve and Paul are okay, but John and Sid Vicious are dolls. Now they try to be more disgusting, but they know nothing about life.

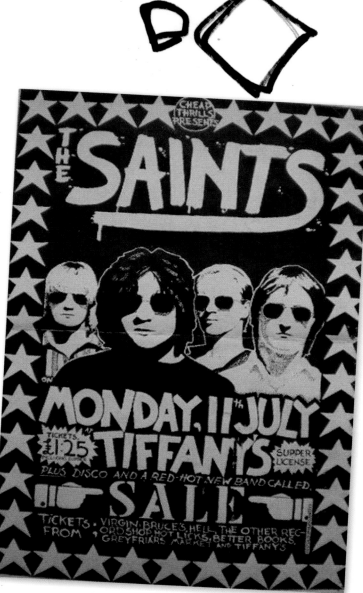

KYM BRADSHAW

The Saints arrived in London in early June and our first port of call was the Roxy Club. We met genuine people there like Mark P and the Captain. We were shocked that a lot of the Punk scene for bands was 'Showbiz' and for a lot of fans just another fashion. In my opinion there were obvious fakes like Johnny Rotten and Generation X.

We played the roundhouse with The Ramones and Talking Heads who were fine. Pity our equipment wasn't. We blew two amps and the drums fell to bits. Looking back now, I wonder if they were really 'accidents'. Also like the time our sound supporting The Jam at the Hammersmith Apollo suddenly went to being good between the sound check and appalling during the gig. The Boys who were also supporting that night walked of in disgust after two songs. I think we lasted about six songs.

The gigs were very hot. One night Ivor collapsed at the Marquee and Chris came back stage and threw up. In Sunderland, we had to cope with Hells Angels carrying axes.

EMI were a shambles. We got onto Top of the Pops only for them (accidently) not make enough singles so we went straight out of the charts.

Meanwhile the atmosphere within The Saints turned truly toxic. We were no longer four mates together. Some egos just went stratospheric and left behind the ethos that originally brought us together.

The rest of them went back to Australia after the tour but I stayed in the UK and worked with the Captain on his 'King' project and recorded that legendary John Peel session. The Captain reformed The Dammed so I started working with The Lurkers. We toured with The Buzzcocks who were OK guys.

But by late '77 you could tell it was all over. The 'wrong' people were coming to shows, you could almost smell it…

MATT DANGERFIELD

1977 was the year that Punk rock broke big and when almost overnight London became the centre of the universe for DIY street fashion and music.

Articles along the lines of, 'Everything you need to know about Punk' were being published, fashion magazines were incorporating Punk street style elements into their photo shoots and photographers, film crews and feature writers were flocking to London to document what was happening. Punk rock was the latest thing

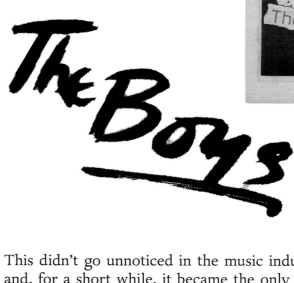

For those of us who had already formed Punk bands and started to play gigs, it was a case of being in the right place at the right time… and we knew it. It was also a great time for the Punk fans who were busy concocting their own take on the Punk look. I knew friends charging foreign news photographers £50 a go to take pictures of them.

The UK Punk scene, which had been bubbling under mainly in London for a few years, had been kick started in December 1976 when the Sex Pistols appeared on the Today programme hosted by Bill Grundy. Clearly unimpressed by the Pistols and their entourage, Grundy attempted to expose them as 'foul-mouthed yobs' by goading them to swear live on TV. It backfired spectacularly. The shock/horror outcry that followed destroyed Grundy's career but put Punk rock on the front page of newspapers, led to radio stations vowing never to play Punk music and overnight made this new movement irresistible to just about every rebellious teenager in the UK.

This didn't go unnoticed in the music industry and, for a short while, it became the only time that artists had the upper hand over the record companies. Instead of bands hopelessly sending demo cassettes to A&R departments, now A&R men from every record company were out in force at gigs desperate to sign a Punk band without really knowing what they were looking for. Within a few weeks, most gigging Punk bands I knew had been offered deals and at the same time new bands were learning three chords and starting up all over the UK and further afield. Once they saw which way the wind was blowing, the music press too was forced to switch from being slightly sneery to supportive. The same was true of radio DJs, recording engineers, venue owners and booking agents.

There are certainly more Punk bands and Punk fans around the world today compared to the early days, but for sheer impact, 1977 was the year when Punk ruled the world.

THE CLASH

MICK JONES

In 1977, a lot of people felt very angry about us because they couldn't identify with what we played. I remember some guys followed us home after a gig once and threw a brick through our window. Things like that were always happening because people didn't know what was going on.

I thought our first single 'White Riot' was a good rock 'n' roll record. There are a lot of good rock 'n' roll records with terrible words – like 'Happy Jack'. And it never worried us that they might not hear our words.

I think back then young white guys needed an identity. We were talking to kids like us who didn't have anything. Those who remembered 1955 were lucky. They had their own music.

Before, it was only authors who made important statements. Music has always spoken to me. The only difference between The Clash and the music of the sixties and seventies was that we were saying it plainer, more coherently. I sold most of the records I ever bought in '77 because listening to them became a waste of time.

The Clash worked on a purely emotional level. We recorded our debut album in a few weeks – it took ELP two years to do their one around that time. They must've wondered what on earth was happening.

All we were saying was, question what you're doing and if the answer doesn't satisfy you, then fucking do what you want. It wasn't preaching, I fucking hate that. It was just encouragement.

The Clash were pigeon-holed – everybody's favourite political band – and we got sick to death of hearing all this kinda crap shoved at us. We weren't 'Top of the Political Pops'. We just wanted to be a rock 'n' roll band. It all got too heavy having people depending on you and expecting so much. We were pushed around when all we wanted was to do and say exactly what we want.

A lot of people at our record company CBS didn't want us there. They tolerated us.

PAUL WELLER

It was either late August or early September 1976 that me and my pals went to the Lyceum all-nighter to see the Sex Pistols, they were on with Supercharge and I can't remember who else. We'd read the review by Neil Spencer in the *NME* (the bible) of the Pistols Marquee show and it sounded just what we had been looking for. The music scene was fucking rubbish in the mid-seventies; culturally barren and no vision or commitment. That first time seeing them changed it for me. I felt that this is our generation's time! It transpired that there were loads of other kids like me and my mates all over the country, waiting for the flare to go up.

The Pistols looked great too; so different for the time with their sound and Johnny's voice, they were something I hadn't heard or seen before. Ever. Rotten was totally mesmerising and had so much front. It was revolutionary at the time. So were the five blues I'd dropped too!

After that we saw them (and the five-piece Clash) at the Punk Festival at the 100 Club. Ron Watts was the promoter, he also ran the Nags Head in High Wycombe. Both bands blew my mind and that was it for me, I wanted to be part of this new scene. I'd been too young to have been part of the Sixties and a lot of the bands I loved had totally lost me. A lot of them had gone Soft Rock/FM Radio rubbish. Too clean, too polished. In the early seventies, I'd loved the skin/suedehead scene, though that was more about records than groups. That was finished by '72 I'd say. Glam had been good but got more and more ridiculous, so from '73 onwards, there was a very desolate landscape. The sixties bubble had finally popped and there was a massive come down.

Punk got us excited again, gave us something that was ours. It was very important for that reason alone. It was over for me by '77 though, once it became a uniform and there were Punk "clone" bands, it was finished I think, though it crawled on for two more years.

It wasn't Year Zero and all that bollocks, it was a generation's time to have their say, that's all.

PAULINE MURRAY

The band formed in late 1976 and the line-up was established in early 1977 with supports to Slaughter and the Dogs and The Vibrators in the North East of England. We were all just turning 19 and our drummer was 17.

Our first London gig was at the Roxy on 9 April 1977, supporting Generation X. We travelled seven hours in the back of a furniture van with the gear. Steve Strange met us on arrival and took us downstairs to the club. It was pretty small and amateurish but the atmosphere was exciting. It felt like all the movers and shakers were there and we had to prove our worth! The club has become legendary and it's great to say we were there!

Everything was new to us that year. We did a residency at the Marquee with The Vibrators, supported Doctors of Madness, Cherry Vanilla – whose backing band was The Police, The Adverts, The Stranglers, Buzzcocks, The Fall. We were filmed for Tony Wilson's So It Goes at the Electric Circus in Manchester and played small Punk clubs all over the country. We were young and fearless and anything was possible.

We recorded demos for Virgin Records and released our debut single 'Don't Dictate' on 11 November 1977. It was great to hear it on the John Peel Show for the first time. All new and exciting!

There was so much happening that year. All the great bands were out and about, breaking new ground. Everything was moving so fast that it's hard to remember the details.

PETE HOLIDAI

The offer to support Thin Lizzy on their UK Bad Reputation tour of 1977 seemed to make sense in terms of promoting our debut album, *TV Tube Heart*, although it would separate us from our own audience and place us in front of a larger, sometimes hostile crowd who had a definite resistance to this 'Punk' thing that was getting all the headlines mostly for all the wrong reasons.

The Radiators From Space were paid a fee of £50 per gig plus backline to be transported along with Thin Lizzy's. This was unusual as labels often 'bought on' to high profile tours like this one.

Not that we had any bargaining power but we agreed to do the tour on one key condition – that Tony Visconti, who was mixing *Live And Dangerous* at the time, would be invited to see us when the tour hit London. Hammersmith Odeon (as it was then) was our preference due to the aftershow party where we could meet the great man in person with a view to him producing us in the future.

Tony produced most of our record collections but that didn't mean he would be right for us. And so it came to pass, that fateful meeting at the aftershow party. Tony was impressed with our vocals at the gig and the fact a lot of the songs used three part harmonies (Phil, Mark and myself) instead of the customary aggressive squealing and shouting associated with the genre.

We were returning to Dublin after the tour for Christmas and Tony asked us to write a couple of 'hits' with a view to recording them and possibly an album at a later date in 1978. When someone of Tony Visconti's stature requests hit singles, you are duty bound to oblige!

After the Christmas holiday, we gathered at my parents' house in Robertstown, Co Kildare, with our soundman Chis Pollard who set up some recording equipment in the far bedroom and had a multicore cable running out the window into a cowshed-type structure separate from the main building where we set up our backline and rehearsed the two new songs we had written.

I presented 'Million Dollar Hero', the bulk of which had been written in minutes after seeing a clip of the film *King Creole* where Elvis was in a boat on a lake with his new girlfriend and she declares, "I told my folks I met a million-dollar cowboy in a five and ten cent store."

Philip presented 'Walking Home Alone Again' and its melodic structure and harmonic elements brought us into our post Punk phase.

We rehearsed and recorded both songs for a few hours until they were in a presentable state and when we left the shed the cattle, that had been on the far side of the adjoining field, had gathered directly outside, drawn to the acceptable racket we were making.

They still talk in Robertstown about the Punk band who serenaded the herd of cattle without souring the milk!

Tony was delighted with the recordings and so the adventure was set to begin in February 1978 six months after recording *TV Tube Heart*.

The recording of 'Million Dollar Hero' took place in February 1978 at Tony Visconti's studio Good Earth Soundhouse, 59 Dean Street, Soho, London. By then, the band had settled in London for the long haul and were travelling from various parts of the city to the studio. The studio was very spacious with a large control room, recording areas and a green room equipped with exercise objects relating to Tony Visconti's interest in the martial arts oh and yeah... A WALL OF GOLD RECORDS that Tony always underplayed.

The equipment on hand was state of the art and in many cases Tony was given use of new equipment before it came on the market. Among the rack of gear was the Eventide Harmoniser, which Tony had now famously described as, "Fucking with the FABRIC of time," as its main function and an honourable ally it proved to be.

THE RADIATORS
FROM SPACE
U.K. TOUR

BLITZIN' AT

4th Oct. Hope & Anchor, Islington, London
5th Oct. Rock Garden, Old Covent Garden, London
7th Oct. North London Poly, Prince of Wales Rd, London
9th Oct. Rochester Castle, London

10th Oct. Nashville, North End Road, London
15th Oct. Marquee, London
16th Oct. Roundhouse, Chalk Farm, London
17th Oct. Dingwalls, Camden Lock, London

ENEMIES
'CUS WE'RE ON THE SAME SIDE

VINYL 45   OUT NOW   Chiswick
                                   NS19

A wander around the studio revealed hidden gems, in particular the tape vault room where this boy would casually browse through tape boxes labelled 'T Rex Get It On vocal rehearsals with Flo and Eddie'. I was in Heaven, Marc Bolan had tragically died five months earlier, so this was the nearest I ever got to him.

If I went AWOL, they would know where to find me!

The recording went very smoothly and we had no problems laying down the basic tracks and key overdubs. For the solo, we had decided to use a saxophone and as we knew Ruan O'Lochlainn, he was invited to play on the song.

Ruan arrived at Good Earth and suggested we play him the track so he could pick up the vibes, while rolling his customary joint. We played the track a few times and Ruan unpacked his sax and began blowing along with the tune.

Meanwhile, Tony had been scoring an appropriate part in notation for Ruan to play. As we approached record ready time, Tony presented Ruan with the written part. Ruan replied, "Sorry Tony I can't read music." Tony was fine with that and Ruan went in and laid down the perfect sax part for the song. I always wondered what Tony's arrangement would have been like.

The mix was finished and was sounding splendid. The label asked Tony to mix a live version of 'Blitzin At The Ritz' for the B side.

A few weeks later we picked up test pressings from the label and from there we went to a local pub in Camden where we bumped into The Boomtown Rats who were hanging out.

Bob Geldof asked, "What's happening man?" He was irked because we got Tony first lol.

I told him I had the test pressing of our new TONY VISCONTI produced single. He snatched it from my grasp and marched down to the DJ and said, "Fuckin' play this NOW!" He stood on the dance floor alone, arms crossed with one hand on his chin listening to every glorious second. As the final E chord rang out he shouted, "TOP FUCKIN FIVE, MAN, TOP FUCKIN FIVE"

Not number one then Bob.

'Million Dollar Hero' was released as a standalone single and had an immediate impact with positive reviews in the UK and Ireland. Karl Tsigdinos of Hot Press declaring it single of the summer! The BBC added the song to their A playlist on heavy rotation and in fact Tony Blackburn brought us in to the BBC to do a session version so he could play it every day as opposed to alternate days which was the rules for a vinyl record at the Beeb.

The single began to shift copies and entered the UK charts at 100, so it showed up as bubbling under the top 75 list that would be displayed in shops.

We received a message from the BBC that if we entered the top 75 the following week we were on *Top Of The Pops*! That very week the label entered a new distribution deal and shops were not being serviced and so we dropped down. Oh well, shit happens.

The label's new deal with EMI gave us more leverage with retailers and they insisted that the song would be reissued a few months later as a precursor to 'Ghost Town'. Tony was remixing the track and I had told him the second verse sucked and I hated it!

Educate yourselves girls, don't leave it all to chance
We can finish early more time for romance.

Although I can now see its potential teen appeal!

Tony edited the 2" multi-track tape and cut out the offending verse and gave it to me. It was reissued and made the BBC playlist a second time, but its moment was gone…

PUNKS IN PORTUGUESE SOCCER FOUL-UP

PETER HOOTON

The Night I Missed The Sex Pistols/The Clash/The Damned & Johnny Thunders & The Heartbreakers (Winner of the saddest title award)

Leeds Polytechnic had a very progressive music policy and me and my mates (fellow first year students) tried to get in to see as many gigs as possible.

I'd seen Spiders From Mars, Deaf School, XTC and many others. It was December 1976 and we were really looking forward to seeing the Sex Pistols who had been making tabloid headlines. They had just released a single called 'Anarchy In The UK' and appeared on the Bill Grundy show that had descended into swearing and insults. The Mary Whitehouses' of this world were outraged but me and my mates were intrigued.

We couldn't wait to see them but then it looked like the whole 'Anarchy in the UK' tour was going to be cancelled. Only a handful took place out of the 20 planned, the others cancelled by local authorities or the venues.

We went to the student union bar and their staff insisted that the Sex Pistols were still going to appear that night. Then we heard reports that the group had wrecked a hotel in Leeds the night before. Ah well, we thought, let's go and see what all the fuss is about and if we don't like it we can leave.

As we sat in the bar having a quiet drink and discussing what time we should go to the gig, a load of loons appeared from nowhere and started pogoing and smashing glasses and acting in a quite bizarre manner. We all looked at one another and gave it that "Let's give it a miss" look. The nutters disappeared to the hall where the concert was taking place and we decided against going and instead listen to Lynyrd Skynyrd (who were always on the jukebox) in the bar.

After a few more drinks, gig goers started to arrive. They all declared they had seen the future of music. We shrugged our shoulders and thought they were mad.

Over the years, I could've pretended I went to the gig and that it changed my life and that's why I formed a band. But even though I wished I had gone, the truth is I didn't. It was one of those near misses in life. I never did get to see the Sex Pistols but I did get to see The Clash (one of the support bands that night) on numerous occasions in Liverpool and seven nights in Paris in 1981.

If only those lads hadn't come into the bar acting like dickheads – doh!

POLY STYRENE

(from a 1978 interview by Barry Cain)

The band had just come back from the States and we went straight into another tour. We kept playing gig after gig and I started to feel exhausted. I couldn't sleep. I lay awake every night, fighting to close my eyes, desperately trying to rest. Everything seemed to be closing in on me. It was all so claustrophobic. Finally, I collapsed and the next thing I knew was waking up in a hospital bed. I'd had a breakdown.

But there were other reasons for it apart from exhaustion. Things like kids pretending they knew me and trying to find out where I lived really got me down. And I used to hang out a lot after gigs. I chain-smoked but that was all I did to calm my nerves.

It's taken a long time to get over it. I haven't played in front of an audience for ages. My body was really wrecked and I still have to take things pretty easy. In the future, I'm determined to be more selective with gigs. I'm not going to play sweaty little clubs any more. I want to stick to bigger venues.

I use my mouth braces like jewellery, complementing my ear-rings and bracelets. I still have to wear them for a while yet.

We all seem to be preoccupied with cleanliness but the type pushed in adverts. A clean, tooth-pasty love is used to sell anything from washing powders to floor polishers. Sex and romance help to sell food - what on earth is romantic about that? Especially today's junk food. I get this recurring dream. What happens when we die after years of eating all this chemical muck and are buried? Can you imagine all the plant life that will grow up around our chemical- ridden rotting bodies? It'll be like another planet.

I guess I love doing different things. I like changes. I like creating images around me. But I don't think I would embark on such a journey now. When you get older, you become aware of the dangers of hitchhiking and sleeping on beaches and meeting different people. I was young and naïve, ignorant of the fact that the world is full of odd people, cranks. Sure, I met them, but I didn't realise they meant me any harm. Simply by thinking along those lines, nothing happened to me. Lucky, I guess.

I'm not women's lib, I'm myself. People have said I try so hard to be ugly that I become beautiful. I'm myself. For some people it's a struggle to be themselves. Sometimes I'm shy, sometimes I'm not the person you see, sometimes I may be myself, but I'm also schizophrenic an entirely different person on and off stage. I used to fantasise at school, and the songs I write now are merely extensions of those fantasies.

I used to hang out, posing, going to endless parties. But that's all over now. Whenever possible, I flee to the country and lead a separate life. I also ride around London on my bicycle, looking at museums and buying clothes from street markets. Cheap clothes, preferably, clothes I can wear just as easily off stage as on. I go for those styles you see in old English films of the thirties and forties.

RAT SCABIES

1977 - The Pistols got dumped, Gary Gilmore got fried and as if that wasn't bad enough, Toto formed.

Fleetwood Mac released *Rumours,* two years in the making. Fucking hell, we didn't even have two weeks, but while everyone snorted coke and shagged each other in Hollywood, our noses were numbed because we were freezing our bollocks off in the icy grey winter that was London.

Damned Damned Damned was released and I took a boxful with me to the Roxy club. It was more than I dared to dream because my dreams were usually on a train that never arrived. But holding the actual record we'd made meant that at least one dream in my head came true.

At least the Roxy was warmer and safer than roaming the streets, well, generally speaking anyway. And at least the punter propping up the bar next to you was one of your own or would at least have some kind of idea as to what it was all about. Failing that, they would pay for your beer while they asked.

But what was it all about?

It's a demanding question and I've had it in the ear with what Punk philosophy was supposed to be and all I know is that it's whatever you want, and if that's the case then it's already yours to do whatever you like with. But don't tell me what to think or how to dress while you elaborate on my bad behaviour. I retain the right to be whatever I want whether you like it or not...

The difference pre- and post-Grundy was that people actually turned up at the gigs. Before that nobody was there. On the Anarchy tour at the end of '76, the only people in the audience were journalists, half a dozen football hooligans and a few blokes with spiky hair who knew what it was. You got no more than a dozen punters down the front who were really into it and they'd get a good kicking, so you ended up dragging them into the dressing room to keep them out of trouble because they were the only allies you had. And that was where that whole freedom of going backstage with the Punk bands originated.

It was a case of safety in numbers. There was less chance of getting beaten up if there were 20 of us rather than ten. You'd let them come in while the local rugby team fucked off.

I felt really let down in '77 by the Who, Zeppelin, the Stones and Dylan. All they did was sell records, which I know is what they were supposed to do, but they sold those records on promises that they were a different kind of people. They weren't selling us the promise of a new album, they were selling us the promise of a new lifestyle, a new future, and when we were 15 and 16 we bought into that. But when I got older, it was painfully obvious this was never gonna happen and they didn't really want anything apart from the next royalty cheque.

One trip that stands out in 1977 was New York City, it was the first time any of the band had even been on a plane let alone fly to a place you'd only ever seen on the telly or had gazed at in *Punk* magazine.

To make it even more glamorous, Stiff had financed numerous liggers and essential road crew to make the journey with us. Oh, and one journalist accompanied us on the plane. He was an unscrupulous bastard who started a betting pool on the plane as to what time we would touch down. He went to every passenger and asked them for a pound or a dollar. He collected the pot and as said unscrupulous journalist was stuck next to me for the whole flight, I obviously felt obliged to fiddle my answer and he let me win enough money for a hot dog and a packet of skins. Result.

The most disappointing thing about that whole trip to the States was walking into Max's Kansas City and discovering it was fucking horrible. I couldn't believe it. We were told it was this happening, jumping place where all the Punks congregated, but it was empty – we were the only ones in there. It had about as much glamour as a public toilet.

And when we went to CBGB's that was even worse. I mean, it had tables and chairs. We had death threats warning us not to go, and to watch

our limey arses if we did. Over the first two nights we overplayed our hand on-stage and the whole thing was a circus. We then decided not to play the game and just play the music and we pulled it off. The Stones, who were in town at the time, even sent along a bevy of topless girls to the club to celebrate our arrival.

The rest of the US tour was disastrous. We went on to Boston and played to ten people eating pizza. Then we went to LA to do three nights at the Whisky-A-Go-Go with Television, but Tom Verlaine didn't want a Punk band supporting him so we were stranded in LA without any money. Jake Riveria, our manager, took us down to the Whisky where Television were playing and we just hurled abuse at them all night – "Get yer tits out, Verlaine."

We went over to America to show them how it's done and fucked up completely. Still, it had its compensations. I remember talking to American girls over there and trying to persuade them to give me blow-jobs on the strength of how big we were back in England. But when they saw the size of the audiences we attracted there, they never believed me. I guess I was pretty insatiable then – but you're only young once.

Wasn't that the point? Life was for living.

RHODA DAKAR

My first brush with what came to be known as Punk was in 1975, at Louise's, a lesbian club on Poland Street in Soho. A close-knit group of Bowie freaks (as we were known) and one of our number, Gill, was from Bromley. She was part of the 'Contingent' that included Siouxsie, Steve Severin, Billy Idol and many other 'names' on the Punk scene.

Who found Louise's first? I have no idea, but Gill took us there and that's where we spent Saturday nights before Punk was happening. I was probably 16 by then, when getting into a club was only about how you looked and behaved. Louise greeted everyone at the door and it was the place to be on a Saturday night.

A few of our group were hairdressers and one, Sharon (the Baroness), used to come round with her boyfriend Ollie (Batcave) and do my Mum's hair. One Sunday, before she left home, we all went round to hers whilst she bleached Bill's hair.

Up to then, he'd had a regular 'do', but black. But Bill from Bromley left as Billy Idol with his signature white blonde spiky look. A real transformation, I thought. Now I believe you're in a band!

However, of all the characters with whom I spent Saturday nights, the most remarkable was Siouxsie Sioux - her persona fully formed even then.

Eventually, we moved on and went to see bands instead. I got to see Gen X and Siouxsie And The Banshees play at the Roxy, along with many others, where Don Letts provided the musical backdrop.

But for me, the attitude that defined Punk started back on those wonderful Saturday nights in Poland Street where "Every little breeze seemed to whisper, Louise."

RICK BUCKLER

When we first moved away from the clubs and into London in 1976, the attraction was the abundance of pub rock venues and the opportunity to play to a younger age group, along with the chance to get out of the Surrey entertainment circuit which, although had served us well up to this point for several years, we had certainly begun to outgrow. We discovered the flourishing Punk scene that was emerging at a few select London venues. It was just what we were looking for.

It was the fact that we played a fast, energetic set of mostly rock and roll standards along with a few original numbers that gave us an affinity with this new crowd. Paul, after seeing The Pistols for the first time, had gained a real direction in his song writing. At first, we did find ourselves straddling the two camps of 'Punk' and 'pub rock' but we were not alone. I remember becoming aware and curious of all the other bands being listed alongside us in the adverts at the back of *Sounds, Melody Maker* and *New Musical Express* while waiting for the next weekend to arrive.

The Punk movement to us was more about an attitude than just a fashion. It was ours – the fans, the bands and the fanzines. The Pistols were grabbing the headlines and the mainstream media was up in arms but we loved every minute.

Interview:
BARRY
CAIN

The Jam – music for today

RUSTY EGAN

I was one of the drummers that The Clash auditioned and auditioned and auditioned - three months in fact. Did I have the right attitude? Was my hair short enough? Would I do as I was told? Very odd that what Punk inspired people to be, individuals, independent etc., I was being told the opposite - you are a great drummer and we like you but you need to agree with what we are about, what our message is, and let us dress you, style you, and cut off your hair.

They were right. I was a mod, a hippie, a soul boy, even a suedehead – at 13, I'd been through them all. But I was really into my drumming. Between 16-19 I played in all sorts of bands to gain experience while I had a day job as a runner at a recording studio.

My wardrobe had suffered as I was a broke musician. I needed Acme Attractions or Beaufort Market and cut that hair but it was too late. My other band became The Ruts. I told them what The Clash told me. I'd been to ten Clash gigs, loved The Damned, The Slits, Buzzcocks, Roogalator, Vibrators along with all the American stuff like Richard Hell, Television, Johnny Thunders and Blondie.

I met Gary Barnacle who played with a band in Dover with Topper Headon. I told Topper about a great band – "Do what they say and you will never regret it." I gave him the phone number Bernie had given me for Rehearsals in Camden. I was playing with Glen Matlock so fuck 'em I thought. I'm not the man for the job but I was for Glen.

By the time Rich Kids got their act together, we were disillusioned by PUNK ROCK and what it was becoming. There were the Sid Vicious incidents, Paul Cook got beaten up, people were being glassed, spat at, fights, skinheads, Sham 69. The message was now OI! – Gary Bushell not Caroline Coon.

The Rich Kids would be different we thought. But after one album and all the attending fights, insults and shit gigs, shit dressing rooms, shit vans and tours, we called it a day.

Punk was, and still is to me, a revolution and I feel like it is so needed today. I am still a Punk, but it's not acceptable - they call it a rant. Record companies and managers control the artists and the media. Sorry kids, your new music SUCKS. I know you think it's cool and your trainers are cool but it ain't rock 'n' roll and rock 'n' roll was 'Too fast to live too young to die'. Many did. Many sold out and became the establishment. Many only had one album - Pistols, Rich Kids and many more. But they had an amazing time. A time that will never come again, like The Happening at The Roundhouse in the late sixties.

The Clash/Pistols/100 Club was the spark that ignited British music and inspired a generation to just do it. START A BAND, A LABEL, A CLUB, A FANZINE! Good or bad people did it. No Bondage Up Yours. Boy, would it be nice to say that to the current music biz.

Can't see Olly Murs doing that.

Pussies.

SHIRLEY MANSON

I was in my first decade when punk emerged as a real force. By the time it started to lose its lustre, I was only just beginning to truly grasp what it had been positioned against.

Initially, I was simply attracted to it stylistically.

In particular, I was entranced by the female punks who looked like beautiful aliens in their provocative regalia. Fierce and unapproachable, none of them inhabited the conventional role of the submissive, pleasing female.

They were quiet and diffident or loud and aggressive and they held their own in the company of men.

I started to hang out with a small group of people who considered themselves punks. They all came from modest, working class families. We were still at school so nobody ever had any money. Everyone shared what they had. Whatever money we could accrue or steal from our parents was thrown into a communal pot and spent on Regal cigarettes, cheap cider and bottles of glue. Getting out of our heads was our main preoccupation.

Buzzed out of my box and with nothing better to do, I started to tune in to the music and what was actually being said by the musicians themselves.

As a bullied teen, singing along to 'Drop Dead Celebration' by Siouxsie and the Banshees, I believed myself transformed into a warrior queen, powerful and avenged.

The first time I heard Patti Smith sing 'Piss Factory' felt like an education. I started to read newspapers and feminist literature. I became outraged by poverty, racism and inequality. Slowly I was becoming politicized.

Pouring over the front cover of *Cut* by The Slits sent shivers of possibilities through my bones and I was awakened.

Everything I had previously thought about the world was turned upside down and I was forever and irreversibly changed.

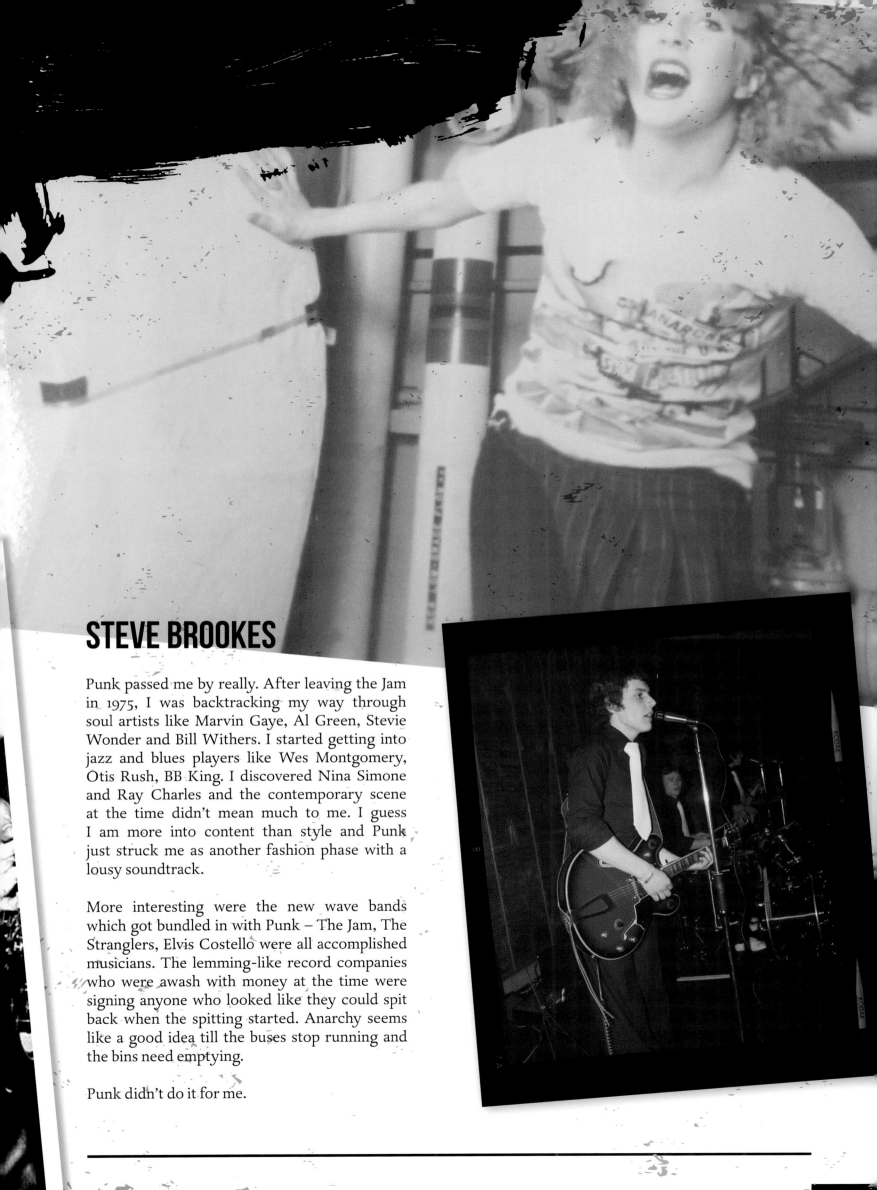

STEVE BROOKES

Punk passed me by really. After leaving the Jam in 1975, I was backtracking my way through soul artists like Marvin Gaye, Al Green, Stevie Wonder and Bill Withers. I started getting into jazz and blues players like Wes Montgomery, Otis Rush, BB King. I discovered Nina Simone and Ray Charles and the contemporary scene at the time didn't mean much to me. I guess I am more into content than style and Punk just struck me as another fashion phase with a lousy soundtrack.

More interesting were the new wave bands which got bundled in with Punk – The Jam, The Stranglers, Elvis Costello were all accomplished musicians. The lemming-like record companies who were awash with money at the time were signing anyone who looked like they could spit back when the spitting started. Anarchy seems like a good idea till the buses stop running and the bins need emptying.

Punk didn't do it for me.

STEVE DIGGLE

The summer of 1976 became one of the hottest summers on record but it became hot for more than the weather. Progressive rock bands had lost their way and the musical landscape was barren. I was looking for that feeling of being young and alive but instead there was coming up to a million people unemployed and the world seemed a very grey place.

I remember thinking of the music I heard in the sixties and early seventies, music that was powerful and life changing. By 1976 it seemed like all that magical stuff had gone. I had a Lambretta scooter and had great times riding about on that until I lost my license and was banned for a year. Grounded. I didn't realise at the time this was a blessing as I then spent more time playing my guitar and writing songs about this no hope situation and a realism I thought record companies and the world didn't want to know about.

Then bang! The Sex Pistols, Clash, Buzzcocks, Jam and Dammed exploded on the scene. It spread over the country like a carpet bomb and captured the minds of a generation. We got The Buzzcocks together and I suddenly became alive, back from the living dead under this great umbrella of Punk. Powerful songs, great art record sleeves and the country for a moment had been turned upside down into chaos!

The power of Punk and the power of those bands back in 1976 gave amazing energy and a belief that through music you can make a connection.

From the first note I played at the first Buzzcocks show that hot summer became one of the hottest years in music.

STEVE ELLIS

In 1976, I formed Widowmaker, a rock band with Ariel Bender formerly of Mott the Hoople of whom, coincidentally, Mick Jones of The Clash was a big fan.

We rehearsed in a dark, dank basement in the Kings Road just up from 'Sex', Malcolm McLaren's shop which I visited with a mate and he always gave me these great T shirts that I can only assume Vivienne Westwood designed. I wish I still had them! We then would go and sign on at the Hammersmith labour exchange.

Widow Twanky, as band member the late Huw Langton (ex Hawkwind) came up with, became our alias. We rehearsed endlessly and got signed by the notorious Don Arden, once manager to the Small Faces and pals Andy Love and Amen Corner.

We were packed off on an endless UK and USA touring schedule. And then there was Punk…

Also in 1976, Mark P, a bored bank clerk from Deptford, having grown tired of glam rock and the old guard's relentless pursuit of the dollar, not unlike most of the generation before, was jolted into action. He started Sniffin' Glue fanzine from home and printed photocopies and distributed then in Soho record shops. It became an immediate success.

Was Mark an instigator of Punk rock? Yes, but there were others. The teenagers were disillusioned with 'No Future' and Punk became another British cult like Mod in the sixties, but very different. Perhaps 'New Rose' by The Damned was the UK's first Punk record but hundreds of these kids were picking up guitars and thrashing out three chord amphetamine-fuelled songs and making their own uniforms/clothes and it shook up a self-satisfied corporate music industry. I, for one, loved the attitude. There were too many bands to name check but the most successful ones were, The Clash, The Pistols, The Damned and in an odd twist The Jam who didn't look like Punks, but in Paul Weller they had a very capable front man and songwriter. Also, Siouxsie and the Banshees and many more went on to achieve enormous success.

The major record labels saw the profit in Punk and got in quick. Many of the other hardcore Punk bands signed to indie labels, played clubs like The Roxy and caused mayhem. But it fizzled out within a couple of years. Sham 69 with Jimmy Pursey, Cock Sparrer, Cockney Rebels and more continued to fly the flag, but the gigs were, I am reliably informed, attended by rival factions and it all got very ugly and totally misunderstood.

Then almost as quickly as Punk started yet another cult was born with 2 Tone and ska, inspired by Jerry Dammers of The Specials that reignited a skinhead and mod revival, along with the Selector, Madness, Purple Hearts and so many more, it lasted much longer than Punk.

I wasn't part of any of this, but I watched it with great interest. My take on Punk rock was that any kid could pick up a guitar, form a band and shake things up and this was ok in my book.

The trouble was, the money men spotted the 'filthy lucre' and that I believe was Punk's downfall, coupled with that famous British adage, "We are not going to put up with this anymore." It sounded the death and it was over before it could blossom, but it will never be forgotten by so many. The record shows that 40 years later, Punk is still fondly remembered with much love and enthusiasm. But with the passage of time facts get distorted and confused and opinions will differ.

So, Widow Twanky lasted a year. By the time we got back from a 14 week USA tour, during which we had a hilarious water pistol fight with the Ramones in a hotel, Punk was over and so were we!

We did however find out why Don Arden was called notorious. He was notorious for not paying royalties to his bands. That 'filthy lucre' always spoils the party...

STEVE RAPID

This was a hard one not to get very personal or emotional about.

Dublin's Burning was the title given to a booking for an end of term concert in the Belfield University campus. It seemed to the Radiators From Space a perfect occasion to showcase Ireland's burgeoning Punk and new wave scene.

So, the band took the opportunity to book all the bands on the bill. They invited the Undertones from Derry and a selection of Dublin based bands - The Gamblers, The Vipers and Revolver.

There was a lot of camaraderie on the day as the bands met and did the sound checks. The omens seemed good. But things began to go wrong during the first band's set. As the Vipers played, a bottle was thrown at the stage. Pete Holidai (of the Radiators) approached the culprit to explain that that was not the way to behave. However, one of the members of this group of fans, being slightly drunk, took offence and threw a punch at Holidai. A brief scuffle ensued but that was soon calmed and all seemed well.

But another audience member witnessed this and followed the punch thrower, Patrick Coultry aged just 18, into the darker recesses of the hall where he stabbed him.in the back. When this was discovered, a member of the Radiators reported it to security and an ambulance was called.

The event carried on with the bands playing their sets up until just before the headliners, The Radiators From Space, were due to play. A large number of Garda then arrived at the venue. The bands were informed that Coultry had died from the wound and this was now a murder investigation.

During the Radiators' set, some of Coultry's friends had pointed out Pete Holidai as a person who was involved in the brief scuffle and in the

July 2, 1977   U.S. $1.10/Canada 60c   18p

new MUSICAL EXPRESS

MURDER AT PUNK FESTIVAL

AT THIS GIG A FAN WAS STABBED TO DEATH

IMAGES OF THE NEW WAVE THIS WEEK ON PAGE 10

light of that he was taken into custody on stage at the end of their set.

All the bands were then confined to separate dressing rooms for questioning. Each member being interviewed separately. This went on till dawn when all the bands were eventually allowed to go home.

It was a traumatic experience which had a profound effect on some people involved in the event to such a degree that shortly after, the Radiators decided to disband. But, after several days and a lot of sane advice, the band changed their minds when they realised that they hadn't been in a position to change anything.

Holidai remained a main suspect due to lack of evidence, but a witness finally came forward and the actual culprit was identified, arrested and charged.

The event was subsequently sensationalised on the front cover of *NME*. It was then tangentially mentioned in the Radiators song 'Enemies'.

It was an event that none of those who attended would ever wish to repeat or forget.

CLASH OFFER -FREE E.P.

STEVE SIDELNYK

So, there I was, going to see my brother's band play in the Ukrainian club in sunny Bradford in the mid-seventies and I was immediately drawn to the loudest and most primal of the instruments... the drums!

After learning to play along to the likes of Slade, Mud, Santana, Be Bop Deluxe and Thin Lizzy records, I was looking to get into a band with friends from school.

It was a tough time with a three-day week and power cuts and the future looked bleak.

My friends' families were working class and there wasn't any money to spare, no holidays abroad and a seven-hour trip to visit my sister's parents-in-law to Devon was a welcome relief from the industrial bleakness of a usually rainy Yorkshire.

I used to listen every night on headphones to the John Peel show and there was a new movement on the horizon.

It was a reaction against the system, it meant that you had a way of expressing your opinion by way of style and music.

It was classless and raw and shone like the brightest star in the night sky.

I was lucky enough to see so many amazing shows when I was 14 to 26-years-old in Bradford and Leeds.

There was the Royal Standard in Bradford and Adam And The Ants played their more times than I can remember in their *Dirk Wears White Socks* period and on a Sunday school night!

Siouxsie And The Banshees with The Cure supporting, The Buzzcocks with Joy Division supporting and The Clash with Mikey Dread and Violation supporting are just a few of the concerts at Saint George's Hall.

The Futurama Festival 1979 in Leeds was the jewel in the crown with most of the Peel listening line-up including PIL.

This was such an important part of my life and it shaped my whole career as every record you bought then felt like the first time you had heard music. It was vibrant, it was sometimes controversial BUT, more importantly, it meant that anybody could form a band and develop a sound that reflected the personalities in that band.

I'm lucky enough to still know most of the Bradford punks and people from local bands like The Negatives and Violation (who became Southern Death Cult) and although everyone has grown up we will never forget meeting in record shops and going to gigs before getting the milk train back from Leeds.

We shared something that I doubt will ever happen again...

TOYAH

On a rainy night in 1975, I walked alone into a Birmingham nightclub called Bogarts to see a band called the Sex Pistols.

I had only heard the rumour about a new movement called PUNK and I was keen to find out more.

That night the music wasn't what it was to become. Johnny Rotten found us, the audience, as boring as hell and walked off after four songs leaving us bemused as to how to behave in such a situation.

I was born in Birmingham in 1958 into a world of Tommy Steele songs and Fanny Craddock cookery shows. My school was single sex, unfortunately me being a tom boy, it was female single sex. I'd have much rather been playing football and war games with the boys.

We had regulation boater hats, regulation cardigans and regulation knickers.

I was ready to slit my fucking wrists.

The weight of other people's opinions being reflected onto me was equivalent to my spirit being crushed by a boulder on a daily basis.

Then I walked into Bogarts night club. Even though the Sex Pistols where on stage I didn't see them. Instead, what I saw was 300 audience members who had all been crushed to breaking point by the same boulder, and we were all about to do a mass break out from a prison called convention.

This is what Punk was for me... it was the liberator.

Punk was both a political and social movement. I fitted into the social side of it. The community was the first time I experienced people listening to my ideas without being openly scornful to my face. Punk was my refuge and my home.

TELEVISION

TOM VERLAINE

(from a 1977 interview by Barry Cain)

The current set-up in Britain with the new bands just couldn't happen in the States. America is so blasé, so comfort-oriented. The vitality and response is not what it should be. Just look at the kind of records that sell.

Over here some people really are wasted, you don't get that back home. Class structure in the States is what's on people's minds – but it's more of an intelligence structure. Regardless of what kind of background you come from, people can gravitate upwards. What I've gleaned from this country is, if you don't make money you really don't make money. The attitude to music here now just wouldn't be accepted in the States. There's nobody around who seems to want a committed sound – they want the wallpaper, not the wall. People wouldn't lump us with other new-wave bands if we came from New Orleans.

If a guy is a good musician in the States he can make $2,000 a week on sessions, so why should he bother to get a band together? What you've got left are guys like me who only just learned how to play. We make the bands. In England, all the musicians seem to start forming bands. I like variety in the music. Anyone I've ever admired has always changed his style – Bowie and Dylan are classic examples.

I'm not saying that *Marquee Moon* is perfect. Our best reception has come from New York and England – your home is where your heart is. It also doesn't strike me as being so fantastically different from anything else. It's all a question of style – and I was satisfied with that.

I guess my desire to do more stuff is greater than my desire to perfect less-recent stuff. That doesn't mean my songs are off-the-cuff. They're particular memories in a lifetime. For example, I like London. When I first got there, I didn't do any writing for three days, then I started. It's funny how people have this impression of me as being a very literary person. I seldom get past the first two pages of a book. Marc Bolan puts references to novelists in his songs. I don't.

I've always been disappointed with the New York music scene – that's why I never hang out there. We all try to keep away from the centre. Besides, journalists make scenes more than anything else. By the time clubs get their reputations in England they've already peaked. CBGBs just happened to have a stage and a liberal owner. To develop as a band in New York you have to play the Top 40 and please the drinking customers.

It's funny when I read about the band in all these papers and the cult-figure stuff. I always seem to forget it. Okay, it's nice to read good stuff about yourself when you've worked on something very hard but it concerns me more when people write lies. Inaccuracy is depressing.

Music is something special and when someone is over exposed to it, be it a journalist or DJ, he becomes jaded. He actually stops responding.

I'm not a loner. You've just got to know who your friends are. Everyone has their own crowd. Birds of a feather. I number Patti Smith and John Cale among my New York friends. But there are certain things you should do on your own. There are certain movies you should see alone. There are certain places you should go to alone. When you find yourself alone you find that you're not. I don't have a telephone because people's lives are centred around them.

hate Elvis

Damned—
om page 45

Seems the Damned and
vis and the Attractions
re returning, by coach,
m this summer's Biltzen
tival. Elvis had got un-
aracteristically drunk on
n i   or to departure
I v   the bus

Ricky, do
lose that
number...

day
tour
of t
stay
"I
tellie
move
aries/
"P
of t
ments
"Do
turns S
God's
n't F

In defence of
Siouxsie
and the
Banshees
By PAUL MORLEY

Just three men: KENNY, JOHN McKAY, STEVE

I WOKE UP one morning
and decided to travel up
to Liverpool to see
Siouxsie and the Banshees
day's rearranged date at the
University.

I travelled back down to
London with the unit and talked
with them. Bassteleven Sioux,
romantic Severin, thoughtful
Morris, cool McKay.

They are not as difficult at dour
in conversation as it appears
externally, but they are wary,
intent to some extent on keeping
mysteries down. Only about the
most trivial things are their
answers definite. Deeper
probing, such as asking them to
be specific about a certain song,
draws a great shrugged response: "From
the listener's point of view...they
don't want to rob them of using
their imagination — and if you're
saying, 'This song is about a boy
next door', then the listener
doesn't have to ponder."

"We aren't read a newspaper.
We step into it the way we step
into a warm bath, it surrounds
us, it environs us in
information," it declares of
[Edmund]
Carpenter]

SIOUXSIE "I never used
to read the music papers
when I was
younger. I used to buy certain
people's records that I like — I
was really used by anything that
critics wrote, I just used to buy

Living in th
modern worl

JAM / THIS IS THE MODERN WORLD

JOHN WELLER: starting all over again

That's John W

Page 66—MELODY MAKER, November 26, 1977

ANARCHY
IN THE U.K.
TOUR

TOUR DATES

Tickets From

FRI 3 DEC	**NORWICH** University	Students Union,
SAT 4 DEC	**DERBY** Kings Hall	Kings Hall, Derby,
		R.E. Cords, Derby,
		Nottingham Record Centre, Long Eaton
SUN 5 DEC	**NEWCASTLE** City Hall	City Hall
MON 6 DEC	**LEEDS** Polytechnic	Students Union, Leeds Poly
TUE 7 DEC	**BOURNEMOUTH** Village Bowl	Village Bowl
THU 9 DEC	**MANCHESTER** Electric Circus	Hime & Adamson, Manchester Virgin Records, Manchester
FRI 10 DEC	**LANCASTER** University	Students Union, Lancaster University
SAT 11 DEC	**LIVERPOOL** Stadium	Virgin Records
MON 13 DEC	**BRISTOL** Colston Hall	Top Rank, Cardiff
TUE 14 DEC	**CARDIFF** Top Rank	Buffalo Records
WED 15 DEC	**GLASGOW** Apollo	Colston Hall Apollo, Glasgow
THU 16 DEC	**DUNDEE** Caird Hall	Caird Hall
FRI 17 DEC	**SHEFFIELD** City Hall	Students Union, Technical College City Hall — Wilson Peck Records
SAT 18 DEC	**SOUTHEND** Kursaal	Usual Agents
SUN 19 DEC	**GUILDFORD** Civic Hall	Usual Agents
MON 20 DEC	**BIRMINGHAM** Town Hall	Town Hall
TUE 21 DEC	**PLYMOUTH** Woods Centre	Virgin Records
WED 22 DEC	**TORQUAY** 400 Ballroom	Woods Centre
SUN 26 DEC	**LONDON** Roxy Theatre Harlesden	400 Club Roxy Theatre

Melody
Maker

COMPLETE CONTROL...

The Insiders...

ALAN EDWARDS

I got to know Andrew Czezowski and Susan before the Roxy as they were in effect my landlords. The building I was renting was not far away at 29 James St, Covent Garden. Now it's another expensive show shop designed to appeal to tourists. Not even a blue plaque!

Then the whole vibe was somewhere between Peeping Tom and My Fair Lady! The streets glistened with rain and the shadows were long. It was a disused wholesale fruit office and I had a little office out of which I was handling the PR for a lot of Punk acts including The Stranglers, The Damned, Generation X, Blondie, Buzzcocks etc. There were a number of other music people based there. In December it was so cold, there was no heating because the electricity had been cut off. We broke up desks and chairs and lit them and made a fire in the office! I know we had an office party there once and The Clash or was it The Slits played downstairs in the office whilst various members of the Pistols threw things at them! Steve Strange was on the door and Andy Czezowksi described this as being "London's first warehouse party".

The ground floor space later became PX Clothes shop. Paul Smith's Floral Street store opened a bit later and Lynn Franks was at the bottom of Long Acre. *Sounds* and *Record Mirror* music papers were above Covent Garden tube station and of course the Roxy was a few minutes away in Neal Street.

Half way up the stairs was Chrissie Hynde cadging cigarettes and Jean Jacques of The Stranglers holding court. It's quite hard to believe that all of this happened and nobody in the media knew about it, but of course there were no mobile phones and camera phones or Twitter, Instagram etc. in those days. Also, Covent Garden was a completely empty and derelict former fruit market and was deserted at nights, not even fully lit. It was still a black and white era and the sense of impending doom was compounded by the ongoing miners' strike, plunging pound, IRA bomb attacks and everything else that was pulling the UK apart at that point in time.

I remember quite a few Roxy nights with Billy Idol, who I'd known vaguely from school. I had been with him when he and Tony James came up with the name for Generation X. I think Tony picked the book up in a book shop and was grabbed by the title. I even managed them for a weekend! Billy, who was by far and away the prettiest Punk of all time, was absorbing all the ideas and style around him before going on to have short-lived success as a mainstream rock superstar in America.

Apart from being a great guitarist, Mick Jones of The Clash was also pretty down to earth and approachable too. I had some good chats with him along the way. Funnily enough, despite all the street cred/ethos, there was actually a lot of snobbery involved in Punk and as always there were plenty of bands and musicians that were cooler than thou. Jones definitely wasn't one of those. The bass player, Paul Simonon, who I didn't really know, was the boyfriend of Caroline Coon, the legendary founder of Release, an organisation that helped people with drug convictions. She was also a columnist for the Melody Maker and it was through this somewhat circuitous route that I helped make the connection between Marc Bolan and The Damned. I was working for the doyen of music PR's Keith Altham at the time and spending a lot of time with Marc who was a client.

ALAN MCGEE

PUNK ROCK 1977/LIFE CHANGING MOMENT/SEX PISTOLS/THE CLASH/ THE JAM/BUZZCOCKS/SUBWAY SECT/ SUICIDE/THE SAINTS/THE RAMONES/ SUICIDE/THE GLASGOW APOLLO/JOHN LYDON/STEVE JONES/SID VICIOUS/RICH KIDS/PAUL WELLER/BRUCE FOXTON/ GLASGOW APOLLO/MALCOLM MCLAREN/ DEXYS/THE SPECIALS/MADNESS/I COULD NOT HAVE GONE FROM LIVING IN A PLACE THAT LOOKED LIKE POLAND ON A WET DAY MOUNT FLORIDA IN GLASGOW TO BEING ME IN LONDON/TO BE ALLOWED TO BE AS WEIRD AS I EVER NEEDED TO BE/ PUNK ROCK MADE IT POSSIBLE FOR ME AND BOBBY GILLESPIE TO BE OURSELVES/ WE STILL MEAN IT MAAAAAAN

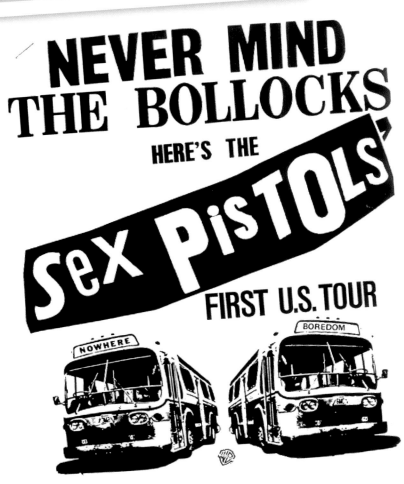

ANDREW CZEZOWSKI & SUSAN CARRINGTON

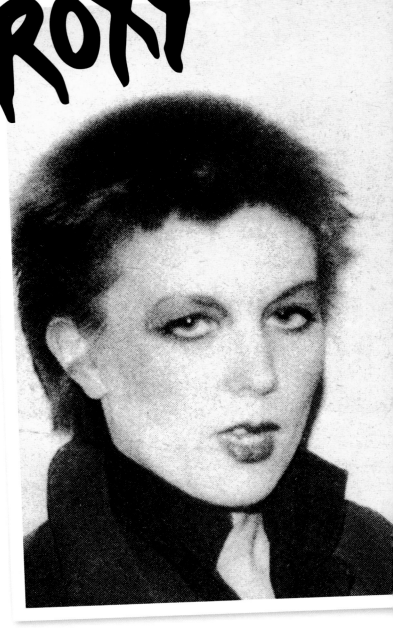

Andrew – No doubt about '77 being the year of punk because that's when it exploded into the media. I paid The Jam a fiver which is probably about as much as they deserved then because only about ten people turned up and it was 50p a ticket.

In our book *The Roxy: Our Story,* Mick Jones says he regarded the 100 nights we created at The Roxy as the era of punk. Unfortunately, the press twisted the whole thing into a negative, hateful, resentful attitude which just wasn't true of the bands at the time. Because the papers created this myth of gobbing, pogoing violence, the next generation of punk bands and audiences thought that was the norm and copied it. It's like everyone is now trying to be a Kardashian.

Susan – I was brought up in Walworth. Andrew was second generation Polish and born in Muswell Hill. We met on 17 January, 1966 during Dream Time at the Streatham Locarno. 'Can't Take My Eyes Off You' by Andy Williams was the first record we danced to.

Andrew – The Locarno was one of the few places that held events for young people and they used to have Mod Nights on a Monday. We've been going out since then. We never married because nobody could ever provide me with a good enough reason to do so.

Susan – We bought a house together in 1971 in Streatham and have lived there ever since. I went to teacher's training college but wasn't cut out for it. At my school in the Elephant & Castle, girls either became a mum or they typed. Andrew and I gravitated towards music and frequented clubs like the Marquee where we saw artists like Jimi Hendrix, The Who, Manfred Mann, The Action and Zoot Money.

Andrew – We went to the opening of the Ram Jam club in Brixton. Jimmy Saville was dishing up flyers from an open top bus with a couple of go-go girls in hot pants.

Susan – The Animals were the first act and the ticket was 7/6. They brought bands over from the US like Ike and Tina Turner, Wilson Pickett. We saw Cream there with only ten people in the audience like The Jam. They didn't sell alcohol. Only years later little naïve me found out everybody then was taking purple hearts. Nobody told me.

Andrew – So that's how we got into music. I was doing odd jobs, office work, decorating. All I wanted was enough money for club tickets and a few non-alcoholic drinks.

Susan – I had a period of baking cakes and wearing smocks. I was a PR at Lambeth Council. Very boring. Andrew and I always managed to get sacked from jobs. I then got a job with Mary Quant cosmetics as assistant brand manager. Didn't like that and hated the brand manager. I eventually got the sack in '74. Then I bumped into John Krevine who owned Acme Attractions in Kings Road. I first met him at Westminster College in the sixties – he had a house on Eaton

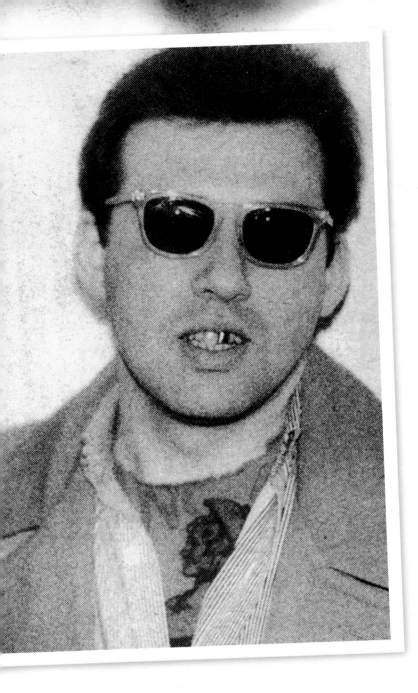

Square and I lived in a council flat but we became good friends. I had long blonde hair, false eyelashes and mini skirt. John sold Americana and bric a brac and he used to import zoot suits, juke boxes etc. Don Letts worked there and it was a real scene. John asked Andrew to do his book keeping.

Andrew – Don then introduced me to Vivienne and I kept her books too.

Susan – Malcolm had gone off the New York to try and manage the New York Dolls and failed miserably. We became pals with Malcolm and Vivienne and saw the Pistols first gig. We saw them play at Hemel Hempstead. Club Paradiso, Chelsea Art College, Andrew Logan's New Year's Eve party in 1975 when Jordan took her top off on stage. It was all fabulous. At the same time, we used to hit Dingwalls and the Nashville seeing pub rock bands like the Pink Fairies, Kilburn & The High Roads and the Feelgoods. It wasn't a case of "We're all going to be punks." It just evolved naturally.

Andrew – During that long hot summer of '76, I was painting Acme Attractions shop in Portobello Road. One day, I stepped outside to take a break and bumped into The Damned who were rehearsing in a church nearby. We recognised each other from the gigs. They said they were looking for a manager and asked if I was interested. They knew I knew Malcolm and Vivienne and saw me as a 'face'. I thought it could be fun and agreed. I had access to a van and a warehouse they could store their stuff in. I have a logical approach to life – I'm there to manage the band and make them money. Very simple. It didn't mean I went to rehearsal rooms or recording studios and hung around. That's their job. You make the music, I'll sell it. But because you're not hanging out with them, they're not sure you like them.

I went to Mont-de-Marsan with them that year. On the coach going over we sat at the very back and all the old fart bands were up front. They were the only punk band there. Rat and the Captain were outrageous, getting out of it and throwing beer everywhere. I thought, shit, I've got another 18 hours of this. I just wanted a bit of peace and quiet. By the time we got to Mont-de-Marsan I'd had enough. I went for a meal with Dave Vanian but the others just wanted to party. The show was a disaster. I got a room in the hotel well away from them but the manager was banging down my door in the middle of the night demanding me to get the fuck out with the band because they'd been creating havoc.

Jake Riviera and Dave Robinson were over there with other bands and The Damned got on really well with them because they embraced the punk lifestyle so it wasn't long before the band came to me and said they didn't think I was the right person to manage them.

I just liked the idea of managing a successful band – a romantic ideal. You then realize these bands are not ready for it because they're too young. In the sixties, everybody wanted an Afghan hound and in the seventies everybody wanted a punk band. Malcolm had the Pistols and Acme Attractions got Chelsea. It wasn't working out so they came to me and I thought, why not. Billy Idol played bass with them and we thought Gene October wasn't really working as a front man so I suggested they put Billy up on vocals as he couldn't play guitar anyway and he had a great image. Tony James also wanted to change the name from Chelsea to Generation X after the book. But just before the switch happened, Gene got a date for Chelsea at Chaguaramas, a run-down gay club in Neal Street. Friday nights at the club was very much the rent boy/gangster night.

Susan – Great fun!

Andrew – Anyway, Gene left the band, they changed the name to Generation X and I became their manager. Susan and I went to the club and told them of the changes but we still desperately wanted the gig.

Susan – But the club went broke so they re-named it The Roxy. It was as simple as that.

Andrew – It didn't matter to us. We weren't involved in the change of name. All we were concerned about was securing the date. What it was called made no difference to us.

Susan – We loved the idea of putting on bands. It was so much better than managing them because they wanted the deals and attention. Andrew and I have always wanted everyone to have a good time, not just the band.

Andrew – So we hired The Roxy to promote Gen X and were determined get the event absolutely right to get them maximum exposure. But because we weren't wiping their arses all the time, the band were getting pissed off and demanding to know why we weren't attending their rehearsals. They couldn't get their heads round the fact that we were spending all our time actually organising the event – putting out flyers, organising staff, a DJ, drink. The show, on 14 December '76, was stunning and a complete success. The band got huge exposure. But they didn't see it like that and ended up recruiting rock writer Jonh Ingham and his business partner as managers.

Susan – I bumped into Jonh the other day and thanked him for taking them off our hands! The day after the gig, Andrew saw Malcolm McLaren with Lee Childers and The Heartbreakers in Wardour Street. They'd been brought over to play on the Anarchy tour which of course had been cancelled so they were miserable and broke. Malcolm didn't give them a penny and they couldn't play anywhere. Andrew suggested

we book them at The Roxy that night, the 15th. We were confident that because of the fame of Johnny Thunders we could get a few hundred people down there. We spent the day doing flyers with Barry Jones, who was involved with us in The Roxy and who looked like a little Jimi Hendrix. He was really creative and the flyers were great. Barry brought all the bands down. The show was a roaring success and they wouldn't come off the stage until 2am.

Andrew – Because of that I thought right, if we can get Gen X and The Heartbreakers why couldn't I book Gen X for the following week with Siouxsie & The Banshees? So we did, on 21 December and that worked really well too. We were hiring it by the day but we were getting tapes from bands who wanted to play after reading all about us in the press. So, we made a commitment and decided to open every night and pay £350 a week – a fortune then. Of course, it was daft idea and we soon realized it.

Susan – After that deal failed we agreed another deal, The landlord would take the money at the bar and we'd take the entrance fees. But it all got a bit messy because they didn't like punk and they wanted to put on a funk night.

Andrew – The official opening was 1 January, 1977 featuring The Clash and The Heartbreakers. But we fell behind with the rent straightaway and the landlord was shouting and screaming on a daily basis making threats of legal action.

Susan – The Damned did a Monday night residency for three weeks in February as they owed Andrew about £400 from his days as their manager. But during one of their shows, Captain Sensible, who's pretty tall, hit his head on the ceiling and a tile fell off so he started to tear it down and then everybody copied him. Andrew had to switch the power off because there were live wires hanging down everywhere. The landlord sent us a bill for £5000 to repair the ceiling. We negotiated it down to a few hundred quid which we paid throughout '77 even though we weren't involved anymore.

Andrew – Miles Copeland, who was managing Roogalater and Curved Air at the time, had arranged to promote a big punk festival at the Global Village and arranged to fly over several

US acts. The event fell through but he heard all about the Roxy and asked me if I'd be interested in putting on some of the bands. So, in March '77 we had an American week with Wayne County and the Electric Chairs and The Heartbreakers.

Susan – At the time, I was working for a cosmetics company supplying Woolworths. I'd booked the Bromley contingent the day after the Bill Grundy for a fashion shoot with top which I presented to the board of Woolworths. There was Generation X pink lipstick, Clash black eye shadow. The board went berserk and I got the sack. Because of that, I got more involved with Andrew and the Roxy and of course, nine months later all the colours I featured in the shoot became popular everywhere. At the time, I used to wear 1950s frocks and plastic trousers with stilettos and mohair and had spiky orange hair. I knew it wasn't going to last but it was so much fun.

Sid Vicious used to hang out in the club. It was like his little family. He was such lonely, sad little character. He used to get so cross when it was busy and he couldn't get to the DJ booth to drink his beer. He'd hide in the booth with Johnny Rotten and drink and smoke dope. That was his little haven.

Rough Trade had stall in there. They used to come down in flares with long hair Fair Isle jumpers. There were lots of people selling fanzines. We didn't have any rules and everything was so laid back. Desmond Letts, Don's brother, was on the door. Spliffs were being sold behind the bar and we couldn't understand why we weren't selling any beer.

Andrew – We were getting so many bands playing that I thought it would be good idea to do an album. We pitched the idea to Mike Thorne at EMI and he agreed to do it on Harvest and not EMI because of their experience with the Pistols. They gave us ten grand and out of that we had to pay all the costs. That floated us back to break even again because we'd been borrowing from everyone including our parents. We signed a contract for the recording even though by then we thought we might be kicked out of the club before we could do it. But we did and ended up selling 40,000 copies. It got to 17 in the charts.

Even though the whole Roxy thing was a success we just couldn't catch up financially. Danny Secunda and Chris Stamp read that we had money problems so they came down with five grand in cash and said we want to be your partners. And we told them to fuck off! A bit daft that. We only ever made money out of the album, we couldn't even pay the rent. We just about survived for 100 days. It was a challenge and we weren't gonna be beaten. But in the end, we had to go.

Susan – On 23 April we were told to leave and never come back. Our last booking was Siouxsie & The Banshees and The Slits and we really wanted to see them play so we sneaked back in but were physically kicked out and Andrew got thrown down the fire escape stairs! We never went back again

Andrew – For the rest of '77 we got a rental agreement on 29 James Street in Covent Garden. It was an old, damp, stinking warehouse owned by the GLC who were going to demolish it. We obtained a pre-development lease, about £30 a week. The band Wire had their management company there, Alan Edwards started Modern Publicity and Judy Totten was based there handling the PR for Toyah and Status Quo. Acme Attractions had a shop and there was a recording studio in the basement. We had a huge warehouse party to launch it and all the bands came. Steve Strange was on the door and charged tourists a pound each to get in and then stole all the money. He had worked at the Roxy in the cloakroom but we sacked him after a day because he nicked the coats!

Susan – Ari Up had a fight with Sid and Andrew had to step in because Sid had a pair of scissors and looked like he would've stabbed her. We had no security and it was a total nightmare. I remember feeling really scared at one point.

Andrew – Oh well, it's all over now, Susan. I guess we were stupid enough not to give in.

Susan – I loved every minute of The Roxy even though I never pogoed, gobbed or wore bin liners…

(The Roxy: Our Story is available via www. roxyclub.co.uk)

BILL SMITH

I was the art director for Polydor Records in 1976 when I first got wind of Punk.

I had been at Polydor for some time and was working on a wide range of covers for artists like Peggy Lee, The Who, Ella Fitzgerald; all very nice and straightforward, nothing too daring. This was, after all the UK arm of a major German record company.

Suddenly, in mid '76 all hell broke loose! The Sex Pistols were making lots of noise and the Damned released 'New Rose'. I went to a couple of gigs, one at RCA with the Sex Pistols and The Clash, a complete shambles in terms of performances but the energy from both the bands and the crowd made it something extraordinary. I'm not sure I liked it all that much but at least it made me think!

Back at Polydor it took until the early part of 1977 for them to catch on to this new wave of music and I had so far been unable to put my new Punk sensibilities into practice. In March or April, A&R guy Chris Parry signed The Jam to the label and I quickly became involved with the creative side. I went to see the band in a pub in west London and was completely knocked out by both their look and their musicality.

My time with Paul and the boys stretches from their first single 'In the City' in 1977 to 'Absolute Beginners' in 1981 and I designed 17 singles' bags and five album covers for the band. Brilliant times for me.

I left Polydor in 1978 and continued working with The Jam, but started touting myself to other labels and artists. I worked with an awful lot of Punk and new wave artists from '78-'81 (all depends on when you think Punk stopped and new wave started). I designed singles' bags and albums for The Cure, their first two albums – including *Three Imaginary Boys*. I worked with Johnny Thunders on *So Alone* for Dave Hill at Real Records, who also had The Pretenders signed – so I designed their first three singles and the eponymous first album. I worked on two or three other singles for Dave's label but the mists of time have clouded my memory and they aren't even mentioned on Wikipedia, so I'm stumped.

During '80-'81, I worked a lot at Virgin Records with bands like Ruts DC and Heaven 17 – my studio created some singles' bags and a couple of album covers for H17. There were other labels and bands as new wave became the more acceptable face of Punk.

First and foremost, I was more influenced by the politics of Punk than the music. There was a huge conflict even within the Punk ranks and I think it's too easy to lump everyone together as either fascists or revolutionaries. But I was anti-Thatcher and pro-Labour (still am). Creatively, I get my inspirations from anywhere and everywhere and I'm very happy that Punk was around because it turned everything upside down – from the mainstream music industry to design and photography in everyday life.

As a commercial designer with my own studio to run, I couldn't just concentrate on Punk and new wave artists, so I started working with a whole range of musicians from Genesis to Richie Blackmore and then on to Kate Bush and Van Morrison. But the creative spark of Punk never left me – I hope!

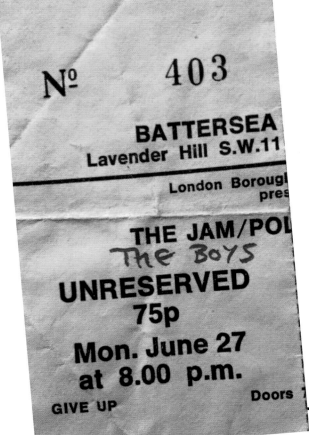

CHRIS PARRY

In summer 76, as a young A&R man for Polydor Records, I came across punk. I was a friend of Jonh Ingham (*Sounds*) who introduced me to Caroline Coon (*MM*). Both journalists were embedded with the Sex Pistols and The Clash but were very protective. I was lucky, I had a car which neither had so I became their driver. I went to all the shows. I would use my expense account to hold the bar. I became popular! I got on well with Bernie Rhodes and The Clash and loved their music too but I wanted to sign the Sex Pistols.

One Friday night in October we closed a deal for the Pistols to sign to Polydor. The band were set to sign on the following Monday. I had booked the Pistols for a week's recording session starting that night. I phoned Malcolm as arranged on Sunday. When I called, Malcolm informed me he had signed the band to EMI that Friday evening, I cried, I was heartbroken, I loved the band.

After both EMI and A&M disposed of the Pistols, Malcolm and I met. He said the band were really pissed off. They still hadn't made a record. He needed a deal and Quick! I went back to my boss. But by now, the Pistols legend had crossed borders and he was told by the owners he was not to sign them.

A few years on I was in Morgan Studios in London working on a Cure track when in came Malcolm who was to follow me working on 'Buffalo Girls'. We talked, we always got on. I had to ask if he really knew what musically he had with the Pistols. He laughed in his inimitable way but admitted he did not.

I did.

FRANK WARREN

When I was about 23, myself and my business partner used to supply slot machines and pool tables to various pubs and clubs. We eventually got involved in running three or four pubs and clubs in north and east London like The Lindsay in Smithfield. A friend of my dad's, called Sonny 'Boy' Turner, and his partner Tommy Wisbey, who was one of the Great Train Robbers who had a pub just off City Road. Tommy wanted to get involved in the music business and Sonny had a nephew who wrote a few novelty hits.

So, one nippy afternoon in 1976, Sonny and Tommy wanted us to go and see some bands who were rehearsing at The Roxy in Harlesden because they knew the people who owned it and he wanted to check them out.

When I got there, the Sex Pistols were on the stage and it turned out to be the rehearsals for the forthcoming Anarchy In The UK tour. The Clash, The Damned and Johnny Thunders Heartbreakers followed the Pistols on stage and we sat and watched them in the empty theatre. To be honest, most of them were fucking useless, but I actually liked it. It was different and exciting and, well, honest, especially The Clash and The Heartbreakers.

The guys I were with were much older than me and to them it was all so alien. They could've just landed from Mars! And when they started gobbing, Tommy shouted, "What the fuck is all that about? Show some respect!"

We went into the main office and there was Malcolm McLaren sitting with his feet on the desk talking down the phone to America.

Sonny said, "Who the fuck are you phoning?" and gave him a severe bollocking. Tommy told him, "You liberty taking bastard phoning America?!"

I remember everyone was worried that the tour wouldn't happen. As it turned out, they were right to be worried as virtually the entire tour was cancelled.

The following year, my Uncle Bob and I went to see Lenny McLean, who was my uncle's nephew,

at Cinatra's night club in Croydon where he was having an unlicensed boxing match with Roy Shaw. Lenny never trained and Shaw caught him on the chin. Crossing his arms Lenny said, "Go on Roy, hit me again," and he did, about fifty fucking times! Lenny just slid down the corner post.

We went into Lenny's dressing room after and told him he must be some kind of idiot to let someone do that to him. I must be honest, I never really liked Lenny. He was a bully. But he was a funny sod.

Six months later, they had a rematch at Cinatra's. Lenny told us that if he won the fight something not very nice was gonna happen to him, so Uncle Bob and I ended up in his corner during the fight. I never knew anything about corner work, we were just there to make sure everything was all right if he won. This time he obviously took heed of what we told him after the last fight and he won.

Later on, Shaw's advisors suggested a rematch and they said we'll give Lenny the same amount of money for fighting, but it was derisory and not nearly as much as what Shaw was getting. I wasn't supposed to say anything but it seemed unfair so I piped up, "Whaddya mean? Lenny just beat him. You can't offer shit money like that." They wouldn't back down nor would I so I thought, let's do our own thing. And that's how I got into promotion.

Bob and I, on behalf of Lenny, hired The Rainbow in Finsbury Park, which was showcasing all the major Punk bands in 1977. The night before the show, Siouxsie and the Banshees had played and the audience smashed up all the seats in the front rows and they had to work round the clock to repair them.

The only money Bob and I made was on big bets. All the promotion money went to Lenny. We had about a 50k bet on Lenny and he won. Then we had the Shaw rematch at the Rainbow and Lenny won that one as well. He got beaten quite a few times Lenny, forget the bullshit that he had 3000 fights in ten years! I ended up putting quite a few shows on at The Rainbow and it was really successful. An old friend of mine with whom I'd grown up in Kings Cross – Barry Cain, who was a music writer specialising in Punk – and I even

tried to arrange for Jean Jacques Burnel, who was a karate expert, to take part in one of the fights and we went to see him on his Euroman Cometh tour to discuss it. Shame it never materialised.

I've always been a big music fan and I fancied the idea of promoting a big band. I was given the opportunity of having Chelsea's ground, Stamford Bridge, for a big fight and doing a concert on the same weekend. At this time, Blondie were the biggest band in the country and I asked Barry if he could arrange a meeting with them, which he did.

So, Barry and I went to the Montcalm hotel in the West End on a balmy spring morning in April 1979 to meet Debbie Harry and Chris Stein and discuss the possibility of them headlining the Stamford Bridge show. While we waited in the foyer as the receptionist called up to their room, one of the Blondie guys, Frank Infante I think, breezed by and Barry said hi.

We finally went up to their room and Chris opened the door. He was very welcoming and then Debbie appeared. She was wearing a white robe and looked gorgeous. We all sat down and as I outlined the deal, starting with flying them over on Concorde, they both appeared really interested.

Then the phone rang. Chris picked it up and the conversation made him look a little agitated.

When he got off the line he said to Barry, "Are you the guy who spent a night on the town in New York a few months back with the other members in the band for a feature in Record Mirror?

Barry said he was.

I didn't know about this until he told me years later.

"Well they really didn't like it. In fact, they were so upset by what you'd written that they've sent a couple of people up to throw you out!"

There was a loud knock on the door. Chris opened it and came back to say the minders wanted to have a word with Barry.

Barry told me after that the guys were really friendly and asked if that was Frank Warren in the room. Apparently, they told him they didn't want any trouble with us but thought it advisable if we left. They then walked away, they didn't want to know.

It was all very amicable with Debbie and Chris but Barry knew the show was never gonna happen now. I asked Barry later what on earth he'd written and he couldn't remember!

I suppose if that had come off my life might have been a bit different. It certainly would've been more fun because I love my music and I really believe Blondie would've done the show.

Mind you, I promoted Frank Sinatra in 1990 over five nights at the London Arena. I met him on a number of occasions – we had a few memorable nights on the town – and he told the best stories in the world. He was as good as gold, and he could drink Jack Daniels like you wouldn't believe.

MALCOLM MCLAREN

(from a 1979 interview by Barry Cain)

I gave the kids something at the end of the day. They knew Johnny Rotten was simply an idea, an idea that gave them the excuse to leave their jobs and have an adventure instead of carrying on and playing safe. That's what they're grateful for.

I set out to swindle the rock-and-roll industry out of one million pounds. I failed. It was just 950 grand. I also wanted to cause chaos. Cash from chaos. I use a word which the British have always found distasteful, exploitation. I wanted to make the show-business world cry. I really took that word "exploit" and bloody well pumped it dry, using it in any shape or form without mercy. I'm ruthless like that.

Every time I came up with the germ of an idea, the industry shook. I created a lot of problems both economically and philosophically. At the end of the day, I made the audience more important than the act and for that I will never be forgiven. I replaced the star with the image and that was the Sex Pistols. I always made absolutely sure that the band would never be stars. When Johnny Rotten took it upon himself to be one I threw him out. And when Glen Matlock left I brought in Sid Vicious simply to procure more money.

Out of all the money we made, only about £150,000 was profits from records. Most of the money was obtained by fabulous advances that I secured from companies at the moment of signing. By the time we brought out 'God Save The Queen', which I reckon only sold about 40,000 copies worldwide, we were the number-one band. We were the great talking point, an attitude, an image. But we were never a band. Oh, there were a few cute songs like 'Anarchy' and 'Queen'. But they weren't important. We were the fabulous symbol of ruin, of no future. The 'Destroy' T-shirts I had in my shop sold like hot cakes – 50,000 in the UK alone.

I know it's been suggested that I'm the big conman of the world. Well, let me tell you, I feel very proud to be called that. My hero is the man who "sold" the Eiffel Tower to a fool.

I'm not a liberal. I love extremity. Most people want you to tear down things. They want you to be shocking. They don't want you to be seen shaking hands with Sir John Reid (then chairman of EMI) they want to see you throw a pie in his face. They don't care if a band can play. They want to know it can't but that it's still up there, on top of that steeple, shaking music by the neck. I never allowed the Pistols to think they were good. I prevented them from becoming stars...'

I wanted to make Sid Vicious a star after I realised people wanted a star. And the last star they wanted was Sid – that's why I would have made him the biggest star of them all. He would have been number one now, had he lived. Let's face it, he had one of the best rock'n'roll voices in years. He had the right attitude, plus the one basic self-destruct ingredient to make him the tops – he never, ever saw a red light. Only green. He would do anything, anywhere, anytime.

Do you know the song I was going to let him sing – 'Mack The Knife'. See, all the songs have been written. It doesn't matter anymore about writing. Just take the culture by its throat, like we did with 'My Way'. He could have competed with Johnny Mathis, Frank Sinatra, Tom Jones, all of them. I wanted to take him to Las Vegas, to let him perform in the nightclubs. But he missed the boat and so did I. I was very upset when he died. Sid was the one to be the star and he was the ideal person for me to abuse. I suppose I was partly responsible for his death. I wish I could've been there. He wouldn't have died if I'd been around. The man had to go and that was what he was destined for.

He wanted to be accepted. He loved the razzmatazz of show business. That's why Rotten hated him. The Pistols were the ultimate showbiz group. After Sid died I tried to promote him as being the Sex Pistol.

I was against the band touring the States. I wanted

them to go to Leningrad.

It's a question of knowing what you're doing. Sometimes you work on your gut reaction, sometimes your intellect. Most times I'm able to combine the two and that's why I'm successful. I can make money, but it never really bothers me. When you're riding on the crest of a wave like I was you get to know when to seize the moment and take the initiative. Like making a record with a 50-year-old ex-train robber.

Johnny Rotten was a good Catholic boy who didn't have the immorality that I possess. He had this silly idea about honour. Kids don't want to be honourable. They want to be destructive and fabulously immoral and at the same time they want to be exploited or to exploit. If they don't have the expertise for the latter they take the first choice. That's why they get onto a stage. That's a tremendous sexual release and an alleviation of all that they've lived through for the past sixteen years.

One of the Sex Pistols' great contributions was getting rid of the music. Kids got more interested in reading about them going up the Amazon with a train robber than sitting in their bedrooms listening to bland old music. It added adventure to their lives. It stimulated them on their way to work.

SEAN FORBES

Swell Maps' *A Trip to Marineville* was the second ever album I bought and still to this day it is an amazing piece of work. When I say bought – I'm saying clubbed together with two of the other Cheddington weirdos to buy it. It was £2.99 which in those days was a lot of money and two weeks of not eating school diners. And that was never gonna happen.

The first album I got was *Inflammable Material* by Stiff Little Fingers and I'd nearly worn the grooves out listening to it on my Dad's stereo with headphones on (it had a few naughty words on it). Because Stiff Little Fingers were on Rough Trade, we presumed Swell Maps would be too. Man, we laughed out loud when we heard it… ramshackle, badly recorded and sounding like it was gonna fall apart at any moment. When it was my week to take the album home, I played it constantly to the point that it was now my first choice over Stiff Little Fingers.

When we heard Swell Maps were coming to Aylesbury Friars we couldn't have been more pumped. But they never turned up as they got thumped by skinheads for squirting water at them. I never got the chance to see them again as I turned into a proper Crasstafarian and the Swell Maps were seen as odd and not political enough.

I still adore *A Trip to Marineville* and the Swell Maps. It's a funny old world as I ended up working in the Rough Trade shop which is a far cry from the first time I went there in 1979 when I thought it was too weird and left in a hurry. Sadly, most of the Swell Maps are no longer with us but that means they'll never reform and tarnish their good name.

Now let me get back to hassling Mute to release the three Swell Maps Peel sessions on vinyl.

NIGEL HOUSE

I still can't listen to *Dark Side of The Moon* or *Rumours*, and it took Jack White to to get me to rediscover those old Zeppelin records. And I still remember Bowie with his wannabe fascist dictator imagery and Clapton with his horrible Enoch Powell inspired diatribe. I am more than happy to stock and sell them (but not Clapton - totally unforgivable and boy do they still sell!) but for me those albums are inextricably linked with a horrible period for music. Too much cocaine, too much self indulgence, too many private jets and separate limos. Too much hanging out with Princess Margaret. I don't know how much notice other people took of Mick Farren's 1976 The Titanic Sails At Dawn piece in the (then vital) *NME* but for me it was the crystallisation of my own dissatisfaction with the scene at the time and it led me to discover the new bands springing up - mainly punk and speed inspired r'n'b. It is hard to imagine the giveaway, ad fuelled *NME* of today ever printing a call to arms article like that now, and you know what, I think we need it just as much now as we did then!

Bring it on.

GABBA GABBA HEY!...

The Deejays...

DON LETTS

So here we are looking back at something you're supposed to look forward to.

How the hell did that happen? Well it's probably something to do with the misconception that 'Punk' began and ended in the late seventies. Now don't get me wrong, that particular incarnation was without doubt life changing, it sure changed mine. I was quick to realise it wasn't about mohawks and safety pins. It was and has always been about a spirit and an attitude, one that has a lineage and a tradition – it ain't even just about music! The whole nostalgia thing belittles what is a much bigger idea, that Punk is a living thing not some weird anomaly of the 20th century. And it's got legs!

Bottom line: Punk ain't something to look back on, it's something to look forward to and if you're brave enough and you've got a good idea you can be part of it to…

DON LETTS
THE REBEL DREAD

EDDIE PILLER

It was Christmas '77 and I was busily rehearsing for my acting debut (in *Henry IV* since you ask) when I was struck down with chickenpox. If you get it at 14, it's not a lot of fun. Trapped at home for three weeks bored out of my head, so my mum's friend Jenny dropped off a box of promos that she had picked up from work – she was an A&R secretary at EMI. She thought they would cheer me up.

She was right.

Amongst the Elton John, Queen and Stones' albums and singles was a small 45 on the Harvest label. I worked my way through the 15 or so LP's until I eventually arrived at the singles. From my regular perusal of *Sounds* magazine, I'd picked up the fact that Harvest was a bit of a hippy label. All prog rock and army greatcoats. I couldn't have been more wrong.

The third single in the pile was that Harvest offering in the weird looking greenhouse bag that they used. It was by a band called The Saints. I looked at the info on the label and it turned out to have been licensed from an Australian label and had been recorded in '76.

I slapped it on the turntable and waited. JESUS. THIS IS IT!! I was gobsmacked. I didn't even get past the intro before I picked the arm up and put it back to the beginning, this time with the volume cranked to the top.

"Like a snake calling on the phone, I got no time to be alone. There's someone coming at me all the time, babe I'm gonna lose my mind. 'Cos I'm stranded on my own…"

'I'm Stranded' by The Saints

That was my Damascene conversion. My life had changed forever. I greedily hoovered up all I could about Punk. I went to see bands three times a week – The Marquee, Music Machine, Rainbow, Nashville, Bridgehouse and a whole host of other two bit venues that are lost in the mists of time.

Three years later I had saved enough money to travel to Australia and follow The Saints around on tour. They were incredible.

GARY CROWLEY

Back in 1977, Punk meant everything to me. It hit me right between the eyes (and ears) and things were never quite the same. I bought into it and fell for it hook line and sinker. I was 15 years old, the perfect age and like most of my like-minded pals, I enthusiastically joined the growing army of teenage Punk conscripts. I was that soldier.

The groups, the records, the clothes, the attitude. I lapped it up. The whole kit and caboodle. It quite simply gave me a sense of belonging and I became a fully paid up member. Quite simply, this was our time.

I was lucky in that I went to school just off the Edgware Road near Lisson Grove which couldn't have been more central, everything was happening just a short bus ride away.

Prior to getting the Punk bug, it was bands like The Beatles, Stones, Who and Kinks who I devoured, reading anything and everything I could about them from the local library. Then one day, the Sex Pistols swore at Bill Grundy on tea time TV and everything changed.

I had already sensed, through reading the weekly music press, that something new was coming. I was a little bit frightened when I first saw the Spiky Tops on that show. They had an edge. They were so different from anyone else I'd seen before. The way they looked, their demeanour, their 'couldn't give a fuck' attitude and their downright disregard for authority was new and refreshing. These days, it's hard to fathom what an effect those choice words from Rotten et al had on a nation. The Sun reported an outraged father put his foot through the TV. Ironically, that was probably more Punk than saying 'shit' to a television presenter, but I digress...

Very quickly the Sex Pistols, Clash, Jam and Buzzcocks (to name but a few) were seldom off my red Dansette record player.

These really were the bands that I'd been waiting for! They looked vital, interesting. and at last there were bands my age who were making music as exciting and dynamic as anything I'd heard from those sixties greats.

Clothes were ultra-important too and because of lack of money it was very much a case of DIY. My school uniform quickly became my 'Jam' suit (with obligatory school lunch stains down the lapels) whilst my second favourite outfit was my white sta-prest, a simple plain grey, weather-beaten school jumper, monkey boots and a homemade T shirt. And that was it. That was my look.

After getting the Punk bug, me and my pals very quickly hijacked our school fanzine and rechristened it *The Modern World!* after a new song The Jam were previewing in their set when we saw them at the Nashville.

Basically, I used the fanzine as a conduit to meet my favourite bands.

My first gig ever was going to see The Jam at Battersea Town Hall on Monday the 27th of June. Seven of my Punk-obsessed school pals and I caught the 16 bus down to Victoria and then hopped on a (appropriately) 77 to Battersea Lavender Hill. I've got the poster for the gig up on my front room wall now. I took it on the way out!

This was around the time of the Queen's Silver Jubilee – The Boys were supporting and we got to the show early, around 6pm. Talk about eager beavers.

We were at the front of the queue and there was a big rumour going around that some teddy boys were coming down to beat up the Punks, which made it even more exciting! Even now, I can remember walking into the venue so vividly. It had big red drape curtains like you used to see in a cinema. My Dad had told me to put cotton wool in my ears as it was going to be loud. He was right.

We immediately rushed down to the front of the stage. I thought the support band The Boys were absolutely fantastic and when they opened with a song called 'Sick On You' I thought I'd died and gone to heaven.

But the best was yet to come. The expectation slowly built and built and then The Jam rushed out onto the stage and it was like "Oh Yes!!" and in

my mind's eye I can still picture that performance now. Them pogoing, bouncing around the stage like demented rabbits as they tore through the whole of the *In The City* album (including the single twice) as well as new songs like 'Carnaby Street' and 'All Around The World'. For me, it was love at first sight.

I can remember coming out of that concert and me and my mates reliving it again and again on the bus journey home and immediately the next day thinking we should all do a fanzine.

Anyway, at this time *Melody Maker* had a regular fact file feature and one of them was on The Jam and on it was John Weller's contact number (I can still recite the number now – Maybury 64717). I immediately called it and Anne Weller answered and I said, "Hi my name's Gary Crowley and I'm starting a fanzine called *The Modern World!*" and her saying, "Calm down, calm down, he's here. Have a word with him!"

I was talking 20 to the dozen, so Paul comes on the phone and told me he that he was going to be up in London tomorrow and to come and meet him at Polydor in Stratford Place. Me and my mate Chris Clunn turned up, me with my flares

on as I was still at school and had no money (I cringe now at the memory). The interview we did with Paul would have been along the lines of what colour were his pyjamas and what did he drink for breakfast! We were aged 15 so it was pretty limited stuff. But Paul was very encouraging, as all the band were. At school lunchtimes, I used to commandeer the phone box out on Bell Street armed with a stack of 2ps and ring up record companies to try and blag tickets and records. It was a very exciting time.

So, our first interview for the fanzine was with Paul Weller whilst the second was with The Clash's Joe Strummer. Not bad going, eh?

I can vividly remember meeting Joe as I was going up to Micky's Fish Bar on Edgware Road for my lunchtime fish and chips – he was coming out of the Metropolitan café.

"You're Joe Strummer! Can we interview you for our fanzine *The Modern World!?*"

"Yeah, come down to Rehearsal Rehearsals tomorrow."

I couldn't contain myself and subsequently

scooted back to school and word soon spread like wildfire, so when we did trek over to Camden the next day we were eight strong!

I was thinking we can't turn up with eight people! But we did and of course it was me who was pushed to the front (as always) and in a squeaky voice piped up to their very intimidating roadie Rodent, "Joe said it'll be alright if we come down!"

"What?! What's this, a fucking school outing?!" he retorted but thankfully he relented and we were ushered in and got to spend a couple of hours with one of the bands that really mattered around that time.

Joe Strummer was very encouraging and we all subsequently trotted off down to George's Café by Camden Lock for egg and chips.

I very seldom ever missed a London show that The Jam and The Clash played after that. They were always such memorable nights. So highly charged and spirited.

London seemed to come alive again in 1977. Despite the colourful, vibrantly dressed characters constantly pushing the envelope, you had to have your wits about you and be ready to run just in case somebody didn't like the cut of your sartorial jib.

The music that Paul Weller and Joe Strummer spoke about being influenced by would ultimately set you off on a musical journey and you would attempt to source those records and see why they rated them so highly.

TV shows like, *So It Goes, Marc, Top Of The Pops* and even *OGWT* were so important because the occasional appearance by one of your favourite bands would make all seem right in the world.

Equally, John Peel's late night show on Radio 1 was ultra-important as he championed Punk and reggae and everything that was cool at the time. Not all of it was great, but a lot of it was. He opened your ears to so many new bands in that famous laconic style of his.

Hanging out at weekends meant trips down to the Kings Road and having the bottle to go into Seditionaries. Acme Attractions, Beaufort

Market and Kensington Market were also places to haunt.

But overall it was about the bands and those records.

The music and the energy that I fed off at that time will stay with me forever. I'm doing what I do now because of 1977 and that explosion of bands and songs.

It's been great the last couple of years to present alongside my pal Jim Lahat our Tuesday tea time fix of Punk and New Wave on Soho Radio. Yes, it's a wallow in nostalgia, but the music still sounds so vital and exciting and it continues to be a soundtrack for so many and influence a plethora of new bands and artists.

Happy days indeed.

MIKE READ

Like the young guys who played skiffle in the second half of the fifties, Punk was a musical revolution that denounced the slick and the smooth to give a voice to young people through a basic music platform.

On my first radio station, I hosted a weekly Punk 20 despite struggling to find 20 some weeks. Bands like Eater, The Adverts, The Damned, The Clash and The Ramones and Richard Hell & the Voidoids all featured, but only for four weeks!

Clearly my boss hadn't heard the show until the end of the fourth week. Bursting into the studio with a, "What the hell is going on!?" the profanities were far worse than those in the chart, but inevitably the UK's first Punk 20 went down in a ball of flame after just a month.

ANARCHY

THRILLS
GOES TO THE MOVIES (AGAIN)
(Well, there's nothing on telly, is there?)

1. BLONDIE

T TIME of going to press — black coffee seeping through the rolled-up shirtsleeves and tired eyebrows — the Hollywood Gossip section of *Thrills* was hanging on the transatlantic telephone, awaiting further information concerning a possible New Wave (late '70s) supermarket American pop dept.) meets New Wave (mid '60s) hyperaesthetic French cinema dept.) schematic cinemaphile's vallacious scenario ongoing osmosis situation.

Because ... rumour has it that Debbie Harry, Chris Stein, *et al*, have bought up the rights to *Alphaville* — Jean Luc

considered for the lead rôle — the more alert lers amongst you will already be aware of the ex-King Crimson, ex-Brian Eno (ex-everything but his) super-guitarist's recent involvement with Blondie, jamming with them on the CBGB's stage during a version of Donna Summer's "I Feel Love".

What with their latest 'Heart Of Glass', 45 swiping the name of the same Werner Herzog German Now Wave film, and this latest murmur, the screen looms large and international for our favourite late '70s photogenic face from the cover of *Cosmo* to the modern Metro.

'The Metropolis was played by

"When I got to the bottom I go back to the top . . ."

April 28, 1979 18p

RECORD MIRROR

FREE LP
Details inside

BLONDIE
5 PAGE SPECIAL

ISSMT WSU

NME VINYL F
The NME Collective List The

ROUNDHOUSE
JOHN PEEL

Virgin on the
ridiculous

RIARS at the MAXWELL (VALE) HALL AYLESBURY
SATURDAY, NOVEMBER 26th, 3.30 p.m.
THIS IS THE MODERN WORLD

THE JAM
+ NEW HEARTS
SPECIAL EXTRA SHOW. 3.30 p.m. UNTIL 6.30
show has already completely sold out in advan
ble now from Earth Records. Aylesbu
Amersham, Free 'n' Easy, Heme
d Luton; Hi-Vu, Buckingha
25p. Usual Friars F

STEPPIN' OUT

DEAD BOY

EMI 2566)

SOMETHING BETTER CHANGE...

The Luvvies...

FRED ARMISEN

Valley Stream, New York 1981 - 1984

This is a suburb of New York City, around 30 minutes from Manhattan. Middle class, with a nice high school, parks and signs for pizza. Me and my friends loved British punk from the late seventies. It was well after it all happened, but somehow it reached us, and we were into it all. The Damned, The Stranglers, The Jam, The Clash, The Specials, the Sex Pistols, The Buzzcocks, Bow Wow Wow. I wonder if those bands knew that they had such a dedicated group of disciples on Long Island.

We had it pretty easy. We had the means to take the train into the city to buy records. We all played instruments and we traded learning bass parts. I don't know why it was the bass for us, but that was the way we figured out songs. My friend Joe was the best at it. 'This Is Wait For The Blackout', or whatever songs we were all listening to.

Most of our fellow students were into music that I wasn't into. It all sounded like the depiction of what teenagers listened to in the movies or on TV, meaning if I was watching a show and a parent was telling a kid to "Turn it down!" it was always a long screaming guitar solo. I couldn't get into lyrics and artwork about wizards, it seemed embarrassing.

I can't remember who got me into Punk. Was it Kevin from Hewlett? He had a Gang Of Four record. Kenny had lots of The Damned and The Stranglers. They all did, I guess. There was Hofstra University's radio station. What worked for me was the positivity and happy melodies. I didn't see Punk as something completely angry. Those tunes were so happy and fun. Everybody's Happy Nowadays.

We laughed at a lot of it, which I think is a healthy way to like something. The American bands were in there too, Blondie, Devo, etc, but something about England really moved us. I really loved it (and still do).

We didn't have the filter of the press, so to us, it was all the same scene. The Jam were the same as The Specials. It was all great, to us. Oh, and Kraftwerk, too. I consider it all to be under the Punk umbrella. I loved how it all continued to evolve. That's my favourite kind of art. It was such a perfect surprise to hear new albums that had timbales, synths, drum machines, and elements of Motown and dub music.

I bought a lot of pins in those days, too. The mod one, 2-Tone... I think you know all the ones I mean. I also had a Mohawk, like Matthew Ashman. I remember one of the reasons I got that haircut was so that when I looked back when I got older, I'd be proud of my former self. That's exactly how I feel. Nice job, teen Fred! I got to see a few of those bands live too like The Clash, Bow Wow Wow and Talking Heads a bunch of times.

When I went to college, I got into many more punk bands. Husker Dü, Bad Brains, etc. But that's another whole piece to write. I just want to leave it at this.

This is easy for me to write, because it all still lives on in everything I do. I am a comedian now, and punk is in all my work.

Why Must We Be Teenagers In Love?

JULIE BURCHILL treks through Jilted John's wasteland

JJ & friend in front room after party.

GRAHAM FELLOWS AKA
JILTED JOHN

One night in late 78 I hung out with Sham 69's Jimmy Pursey in his London hotel. I can't remember why I was there or any details except Jimmy proudly showing me an expensive new shirt and pair of slacks he'd just bought.

He then refolded them carefully and placed them in a smart sports bag (also new) before his girlfriend rang on the hotel phone and he became deeply immersed in conversation. He appeared to be placating her, telling her how much he was missing her and getting just a little bit soppy. I think at the time Sham 69 were riding high in the charts with the macho anthem 'Hurry Up Harry', and it amused me how at odds that song and the band's image were with what I was witnessing – an emotional outpouring from a very well-groomed and emotionally sensitive man. Not very Punk, I thought.

But then, in reality, Punk Rock as a political statement was on the wane and disco was all the rage. Indeed, with his smart hair and if his new clothes had been cut a little differently, I believe Jimmy could have slipped off into a nightclub and danced the night away to the Bee Gees, and would have fitted in perfectly.

At the time, my brief moment of pop stardom was already behind me. My one hit single 'Jilted John' had dropped out of the charts weeks before, and I had returned to my drama school studies in Manchester, spending tedious hours standing in a loincloth wearing a cardboard Greek theatrical mask and chanting, "Agamemnon, Agamemnon!"

How I envied Jimmy Pursey who was still enjoying his 15 minutes of fame. I felt the same envy when years later a pissed Vic Reeves told me he'd been offered fifty grand to appear in a ketchup commercial, and he was thinking of turning it down. Fame is such a fickle beast, and Jimmy famously and wisely once said, "I was on the scrap heap five years ago, and in another five I'll be back there" I lost track of his career, so I don't know if that actually happened. I hope not, and I hope he sorted things out with his girlfriend.

MARTIN FREEMAN

Some memories from my very young childhood:

Wetting my hair in the bathroom, trying to spike it up like Paul Simonon, then denying it when Laura asked me what the hell I thought I was doing.

Hearing the opening guitar riff of 'Pretty Vacant' and giving it my best demonic stare which I thought would impress my Tim and Jamie.

Being amazed when I first heard people say "fuck" on records, and hoping my Dad would never hear them being played in our house.

Listening to Live At The Electric Circus and hearing proper North-West accents sounding bored and mean and deranged at the same time.

Having 999's 'Nasty Nasty' blazing through my head as I walked round the estate, feeling invincible.

All these names were fun and threatening – Rotten, Vicious, Rat, Ian Dury…The Guildford Stranglers? That's not far from us, right?

Drawing pictures of bands on little pieces of card – The Jam, The Clash, The Pistols.

And Tom Petty and the Heartbreakers; they were allowed, too.

Learning what 'pogoing' was. Tim showing me what it looked like.

I wasn't a Punk. I was a five and six-year-old boy. But this stuff was important. I loved it. I still do.

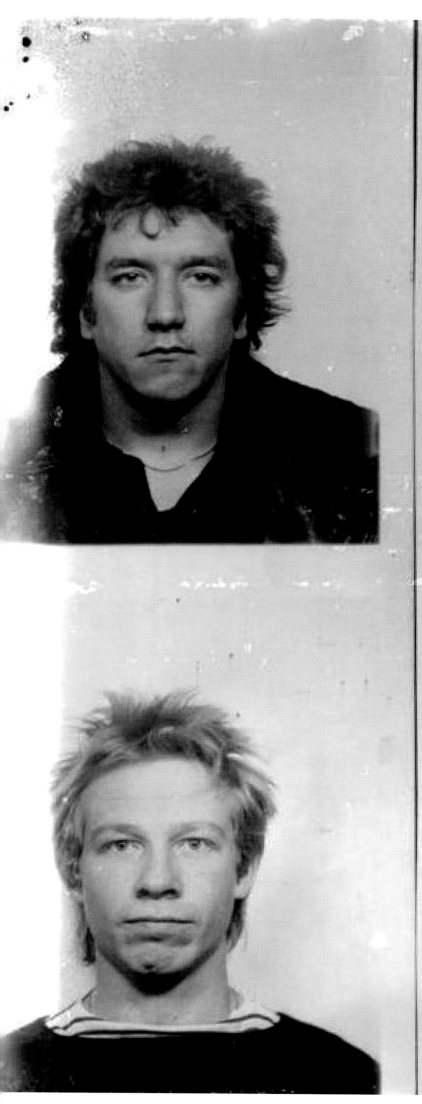
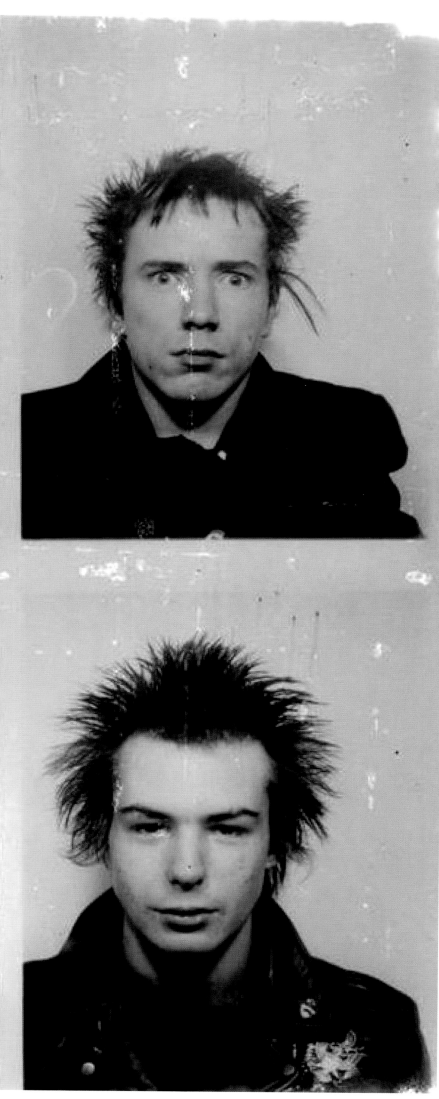

BBC place TV and radio ban on new single

exclusive 15 month contract by appearing on tour for another promoter.

Diamond drug charge dropped

NEIL DIAMOND, who last June was arrested and charged on possession of under an ounce of

NOEL REDDING and two members of his band, David Clarke and Leslie Sampson, are taking High Court action over a record and management deal.

They are claiming damages and relief from Jonathan Brewer and Robert Patterson, directors of Anastasia Promotions Ltd. The three musicians claim they signed a deal with the two men for a company called Diamond Records in June 1975. They want a

quits

EATER'S 15 - year - old left the band because of But Dee is to form a next week.

THE BBC have banned the Sex Pistols, as their single, 'God Save The Queen', im... straigh...

always been politically di... and socially outspoken. As it happens... has ge...

Mirror, May 7, 1977

CLASH

PISTOLS

DAMNED

Rock fan's pub death: two charged

TWO MEN have been sent for trial at the Old Bailey following the death of rock fan Henry Bowles, who was pushed through a plate glass window at the Bell pub in Pentonville road during a gig on October 23. He died in hospital two weeks later without regaining consciousness.

manslaughter and Frank Flood, aged 22 from Islington, is accused maliciously causing grevious bodily harm.

The two men were sent for trial after a hearing at Clerkenwell Magistrates Court and released on £500 bail each with a similar s

STRANGLERS

JAM

THE ADVERTS

On tour with the Damned
Single out now BUY 13
One Chord Wonders

Dee Generate has
differences. ''
and is auditioning

GE
ENIES
RUG
WOOP

EWSPAPER report
Moody Blues drum-
Graeme Edge was
ht up in a drugs
p has been emphat-
y denied by Edge and
ecord company.
e story told of a drugs
on the yacht Delia in
fax, Nova Scotia, and
£8 million worth of
abis was found on
·d — about six tons
h.
press statement from
ca Records however
ns that Edge is now
g - in the South of
nce as a tex exile, and
the Delia was once

NEAT NEAT NEAT...

The Writers...

ADRIAN THIRLLS

"The live gigs are where it all happens, so what are you complaining about?"

So began my journalistic career in 1976 – and it was all about punk. I chronicled the first year or so of the punk explosion in my fanzine *48 Thrills*, and my abiding impression of those heady days, especially the months before the private party turned into a national phenomenon, was of just how young and innocent the whole shebang was.

The mainstream media portrayal of punk as a violent and nihilistic time was astonishingly wide of the mark. Sure, there was plenty of snarling – though not so much spitting as you were subsequently led to believe – and a simmering resentment at the lack of good times and opportunities available in grey, lacklustre seventies London. But the mood of early punk was overwhelmingly upbeat. It was an energetic roar against apathy. "This is generation positive rather than generation blank," Billy Idol told me. "That whole blank generation thing is more American."

The first punk gig I saw was the Sex Pistols at the 100 Club that summer. Some weeks later, I caught the Pistols there again, this time with The Clash, then a five-piece playing their third public gig, as the support band. Gigs by The Jam, The Damned, Subway Sect, The Slits, Buzzcocks, Generation X and Siouxsie & The Banshees soon followed, although the scarcity of venues happy to host that first wave of groups meant that there would rarely be more than one punk gig a week. But, with the same, invariably friendly, faces cropping up at every show, I quickly felt a sense of camaraderie.

As a suburban teen who had been into funk and soul until that point, the noisy aggression of punk guitars, in particularl the heavy metal thunder mustered by the Sex Pistols, initially came as a shock. Once I'd grown used to their rawness and lack of a dance groove, though, those guitars became the soundtrack to my late teens.

The early punk musicians were on the cusp of becoming stars, but the connection between the bands and their audience was real. I can remember long conversations with Mick and Paul of The Clash on the stairs leading down to the 100 Club basement. And of being inspired to make my first, home-sprayed, red-green-and-gold shirt with the phrase 'Danger Stranger' scrawled on it a few days later. Of hooking up with Shane MacGowan and Claudio 'Chaotic Bass' Magnani and together concocting our own variation on punk style by adding white, Sta-Prest jeans and shirts and ties. "Looking scruffy is conforming," said Shane. It wasn't all safety pins and ripped clothes. At the start, punk was far more individualistic in terms of style.

The groups helped out with the mag, too. Not just with interviews and guest lists. They physically helped to put the thing together. I collated one issue while The Jam were recording the brilliant 'Away From The Numbers' in Stratford Place, just off Oxford Street. Hundreds of sheets of paper were strewn over the studio floor as Paul, Bruce, Rick and I sorted them out. The Clash also embraced that all-for-one ethos, always ready to offer a floor to sleep on if I was stranded. Despite the rhetoric, the early punks were essentially peaceful, although the same couldn't be said of London in '76 and '77. You would fear for your safety on tubes and buses. Wearing full Clash City Rockers regalia, I was attacked by teddy boys on the escalator at King's Cross tube station. A few months later – irony of ironies – me and some of the usual suspects, sporting a more mod-inspired look, were set upon by a gang of Johnny-Come-Lately parody punks in Mohawks on the Euston Road.

The private party soon ended, of course. Some bands burnt out. Others continued to make great music but entered the mainstream. I did the same, putting *48 Thrills* to bed after six issues and moving over to write for the *NME*. Mick Jones told me, early on, that things would never be the same as in the early days. He was right, of course – but it was glorious while it lasted.

ALAN BUTCHER

I had always been a rock fan and had bought import albums of the New York Dolls. Then I saw Iggy of The Stooges at Kings Cross. Amazing. The Ramones album came out and I loved the short songs with Johnny Ramone's guitar thrashing. I heard about The Sex Pistols and The Damned and got to see them at the 100 Club. I was hooked. I got rid of a couple of my more boring girlfriends and jumped in. I started my fanzine, *LiveWire* after seeing *Sniffin' Glue* and *48 Thrills.* I went to every record shop that dealt with Punk and old garage band stuff. I saw bands every night. The Damned and The Boys at The Hope & Anchor, Chelsea with Billy Idol at the Nashville, Vibrators and The Jam at the 100 Club, Then came The Clash and I went to Harlesden as well as many more gigs. I got to meet and know all the bands. These people had similar tastes to my own. I gave up the day job in an office to concentrate on pushing my fanzine. I hung out at Rough Trade records. I found new girls to hang out with. I later wrote for Zigzag magazine and Kris Needs called me his man on the streets. I met my wife after asking her to pose with me on a record I made with members of The Boys and Bernie Torme Band. Paul Weller came to my house when I was living with my parents in South London. I had no brothers or sisters so girls slept with me and other music followers and some musicians slept on my floor. It was the most exciting time of all for me. I loved The Damned, Clash, Jam, Pistols, Boys and Lurkers. I often got up and sang with the Boys and Lurkers onstage. Honest John was my best man and is in the wedding photos So are the Boys, Lurkers, Members, etc. I got to be a tour manager with The Boys and managed a Punk band called Defiant. I got up onstage at The Roxy when Dave Vanian was not around. I only knew one song – New Rose. It was fun. I used to hang out with Shane and Shanne of The Nips in those days. I used to get a bus to Croydon and drink with Rick Buckler and Captain Sensible.

ALF MARTIN

It was Queen that started it.

Thames Television had the band booked to appear on the Thames Television's Today show on 1 December 1976. For some reason, Freddie Mercury and the rest of Queen couldn't appear. Fellow EMI artists The Sex Pistols turned up to replace them with an entourage from the Bromley Contingent, including Siouxsie Sioux, who were all offered drinks before going on air.

It's fair to say there was a bit of swearing and silliness between the band and the programme's host, Bill Grundy.

After the show, all hell ensued. Viewers complained, Grundy was suspended and the newspapers went to town. "The Filth and the Fury" was the *Daily Mirror's* front page headline. "Four Letter Words Rock TV" claimed the Daily Telegraph.

The Pistols and Punks became the zeitgeist of music. They set off on the Anarchy In The UK tour with The Clash, Johnny Thunders' Heartbreakers and The Damned (later thrown off by Malcolm McLaren)

Local authorities, the media, Welsh carol singers, a preacher and packers at an EMI plant were in uproar. The tour lasted for about six dates.

Glen Matlock left the band, Sid Vicious replaced him. EMI pulled, A&M signed and sacked them within days and Virgin jumped in. *Never Mind The Bollocks* followed but a tour of the UK proved impossible at that point, so they flew to the Netherlands for secret dates.

"No-one else knows where they are but if you get over to Sweden and meet up with the band's tour manager, he'll sort you out," said Virgin's PR Al Clarke.

An exclusive. A flight, then a very slow, nine-hour train ride and, being so late, a missed gig in the depths of the wilderness.

So, it's a flight on a very small plane and a pilot, who looked about 18, with Sid sitting next to him in the co-pilot's seat along with numerous substances. "Let's have a go," giggled Sid as we flew to their next destination. And he did. The band's roadie, Rodent, who also worked with The Clash, looked scared. I tried to keep calm when Sid said, "Can it do a loop-de-loop?"

Steve Jones and Paul Cook have gone by road to the next gig at Barbarella's in Vaxjo. Steve stating later he refuses to fly with, "a pilot who's a nutter. I always go in the van."

Tonight, Saturday, halfway through their tour in an industrial town of car factories and showrooms, the band are playing in, what looks like, a works community centre, next door to a Fiat warehouse.

Four cops, with huge batons and guns, are at the doorway, turning away anyone who looks under age.

Backstage I can hear Johnny shouting at the DJ to put some reggae on. The DJ answers the call and Johnny's up and dancing. He opens the dressing room door to get the full volume. "Now that's music," he says, "Tell them we'll be on in ten minutes."

I'm positioned by the sound engineer, standing on a chair, when a girl of about 17 asks if I'm with the band. "Yes, sort of," and she goes straight to my flies and pulls the zip down. There's at least 300 kids around us but she has no inhibitions. I have.

"It's great to be playing, that's what we're in a band for," says Rotten. And they're away. The kids love it. Eventually, after a lot of goading from Rotten, dancing to songs they've never heard, continually shouting for 'God Save Queen', which is No.8 in the Swedish charts. "You'll have to wait, it comes at the end." They finally get what they asked for. Johnny's orange hair bobbing all over the place with the words "No future" repeated over and over. After an encore, they return to play their current single in the UK, 'Pretty Vacant'. Soon after Sid joins me at the sound engineer's desk and asks for copies of the recorded gig, which he immediately tries to sell. Unfortunately, I didn't buy one.

Next morning in the hotel restaurant, that has coffee machine style confusion for ordering food. Out pops a ticket with a number on it. Steve Jones is at a table waiting for his order that he's not sure if it's what he actually wanted. It turns out to be frankfurter and chips.

"It's so boring this country," he says, "Nothing to do, nowhere to go. They've even got strange drinking laws."

While we're sitting and chatting, in walks the past, those 'Hippy Hippy Shake' boys from the swinging sixties, the Swinging Blue Jeans. "Those kind of bands usually play residencies here," Steve says, "it must be really boring. It's bad enough one or two nights in one place. They've been playing here for about two months. I wanna get back to Britain. If only we could play there."

Later, at lunchtime, there's an endless queue to fill rumbling stomachs. All trying to work out the menu. You pick the one you want, press a button and when you get to the end the grub is ready. No it isn't. Johnny, Paul and Sid have ordered No.3. They think it's steak, potatoes and mushrooms. It turns out to be fish. "It tastes like cardboard," says Johnny, but devours it anyway. "It's all plastic, everything's so bland. We think it's bad being poor but if this is what money brings, I don't want it."

Sid missed breakfast and the waitress arrives with his order of yoghurt, a bowl of cornflakes, the fish, a glass of milk, a Coke and strawberries. He decides it's awful and mixes it all up on one plate and tucks into the mess but gives up after a few mouthfuls.

Sound-check in the afternoon and into the van. Not enough seats for all of us and I've decided I'm not being left behind so I sit on Rotten's lap, who keeps moaning I'm a fat fucker.

It's snowing outside, there's nothing to do, nowhere to go. Virgin has organised for the Swedish press to meet at a restaurant for a slap-up meal.

The menu is in three different languages, so no worries about what they're ordering. Johnny and Sid want escargot and onion soup to start with. Rodent wants caviar.

A Swedish journalist asks Johnny something and he loudly proclaims, "We want freedom, freedom for everybody, to say and do what they want. We don't want anyone telling us what to do."

On to the main course and Rodent has ordered steak. He lifts it off his plate with his hands and stuffs it in his mouth. It makes a nice picture for the Swedish photographers, who probably think he's a member of the band.

Ice cream to finish and it's back to the club for the second gig at the venue. On the way, Sid's worried about his UK court appearance for drug offences a couple of days later. "Has anyone got a suit I can borrow?" I wonder if he's serious. Luckily, I'm shorter and fatter than him.

It's a smaller crowd tonight. Rotten looks like a waif left over from the *Oliver* film. The DJ has got the message and is playing Johnny's personal reggae tapes. Then the band are straight onto the stage and into 'Anarchy In The UK'.

Rotten's hanging onto the mike, using it as a crutch so he won't fall over the edge of the stage. They're playing much better than the previous night. Paul and Sid working well together. Steve, legs splayed, playing like a demon and Johnny rearranging his hair as though he's frightened he'll get the Brylcreem look. "I'm getting bored," he screams. He leans on the monitors as though he's exhausted. The set is like last night's gig, finishing this time with 'No Fun'.

Back in the dressing room Johnny's not happy. He couldn't hear what he was singing but the rest of

the band know they played much better. He just hides his head under a towel.

Autographs are signed, drinks are drunk and it's back to the hotel. The van's windscreen has been sprayed with paint, names have been scratched on the side of the van and the fan belt's been cut but we can still drive the short distance back. I'm on Johnny's lap again in the front seat. He's paranoid about people following us. He's frightened the local lads are out to get him. "It's not as bad here as in London," he says, "but they carry six inch knives here."

The next day I'm on my way back to the UK. The band have got two days to fill while Sid appears in court. He's standing in reception with the youthful but manic looking pilot and asks if I want to fly back to Britain with them. I make my excuses, run to my taxi to take me to the station and an interminable 500-mile train ride to Stockholm, flying safely home with an exclusive

for *Record Mirror*.

PS: The Swinging Blue Jeans, no original members, are still doing the 'Hippy Hippy Shake' on UK tours with other sixties artists.

DAVID BROWN

Yes, 1977 will always be remembered as the year of Punk rock but that didn't mean that existing bands just laid on their backs and kicked their legs in the air. Far from it; for most it was business as usual.

The most successful album of the year worldwide was Fleetwood Mac's *Rumours*, while the best-selling single was 'Hotel California' by The Eagles. Not content with spending 31 weeks at the top of the US album charts, four single tracks taken from *Rumours* made the American top ten. To this day, radio stations on both sides of the Atlantic continue to play those tunes by The Eagles and Fleetwood Mac to death.

While it may not have received instant recognition upon its release in January 1977, David Bowie's *Low* has been critically reappraised and this step into the world of avant garde electronics is now seen as one of his best. Though mostly recorded in France, it is known as the first part of what's been labelled his 'Berlin trilogy' working with producer Tony Visconti and Brian Eno.

Pink Floyd could in no way be thought of as angry young men but their message was clear enough in *Animals* (you know, the one with the flying pig over Battersea power station), that they were not happy about what was going on in the world. Many found this concept album hard work, but it proved that you didn't have to be a Punk to make your social-political point.

Following the release of *Sneakin' Suspicion*, Wilko Johnson said a quick "See you later" to Dr Feelgood because of differences of opinions with singer Lee Brilleaux, who brought in John 'Gypie' Mayo on guitar and the band played on.

The year saw a sad departure for Elvis Presley in August, Marc Bolan would boogie no more following a car crash in September, while an air crash the following month claimed three members of US Southern rock specialists Lynyrd Skynyrd just days after the release of their *Street Survivors* album.

Traditional rock & roll was far from dead. Long live rock & roll...

EUGENE BUTCHER

I was a 15-year-old budding skateboard king, living the dream in New Zealand in 1977.

Thin Lizzy were my favourite band, but that golden year the zeitgeist of Punk was about to change and shape my life forever.

It was a spotty English kid at school called Nathan Bird that introduced me to the first of the great albums of 1977 that were the start of my loud n' proud awakening – The Stranglers mighty *Rattus Norvegicus*. I was immediately hooked and The Damned, Saints, and The Clash debuts were soon my favourite new records.

So many great, epic and legendary Punk albums dropped in 1977 and a couple of the greatest rock records – AC DC's *Let There Be Rock* and Thin Lizzy's *Bad Reputation* which both had a Punk feel.

It was a year of quality. Imagine getting all these

albums released in 2017. It would be incredible! Shortly after, my transformation began. The hair was cut, my grandad's suit jackets were modified, the sneakers had chequers drawn on them. And then we formed our first band - the nihilistic sounding THE PRODUCTS. Covers were soon learnt, originals written and before we knew it, we played our first gig.

Then we started promoting shows in church halls and designing posters – it was a rush of creativity and excitement the likes of which I would never feel quite as much again. My band did become pretty famous back in New Zealand.

Since then, I've continued to play in bands, set up a record label and now make a living out of publishing magazines documenting Punk rock like *Vive Le Rock*. That year shaped my politics and world view and made me friends for life. So, 1977 – No Future? Nah, not for me. It was my chance and I took it.

GARRY BUSHELL

Jumbo flares, Concorde collars, inflation, perms, the Brotherhood of Man, rising youth unemployment, Denis Healy cutting billions in return for an IMF loan…

The Britain of 1976 was curling up at the edges.

England suffered the worst drought on record, but that was nothing compared to the drought in popular culture. The charts were dominated by Tina Charles, Abba and the Wurzels. Glen Campbell had an album at number one for six sodding weeks. The likes of Yes, Genesis and ELP were still hanging about like unwanted turkey two days after Christmas.

And the rock press was into Chic Corea, Al Di Meola and Weather Report – superb musicians who couldn't write a decent song between them. No fun, my babe, no fun…

Punk cut through all that bland or pretentious cobblers like a Stanley knife; all these wild-eyed kids, cranked-up really high, bursting with energy and attitude.

Joe Strummer changed my life, literally. If it hadn't been for The Clash, I would never have started down the route that led to a job on Sounds.

I wouldn't have reformed my band, or started a fanzine. I might not even have become a writer.

I remember defending Punk in the *Socialist Worker* from those who couldn't see past McLaren's dodgy swastika shock tactics… buying The Damned's 'New Rose' single on the day it came out in October '76 at a record shop (remember them?) in Shepherds Bush… watching Bill Grundy's road-crash Sex Pistols interview live on ITV.

It was the most exciting television since Slade's debut with 'Get Down & Get With It' in the same tea-time time-slot five years earlier.

Over the coming months, I saw Gen X at Barking, The Stranglers at the Roundhouse, The Damned supporting T Rex…

But for me the greatest gig of 1977 was The Clash, The Jam, Buzzcocks and Subway Sect at the Rainbow in Finsbury Park. What a line-up! What a night!

It was part of the White Riot tour and the audience made the papers for allegedly causing £1000 worth of damage by ripping up some seats. But it wasn't 'a riot', as some papers reported, more genuine excitement – some of those chairs just collapsed under the pogoing.

All the first-generation Punk bands released albums in 1977. *The Clash* by The Clash was my first love, the one I could still recite every word of. I still love their early, raw, exuberant rage.

It's harder to pick a single of the year; there was so much classic vinyl around. The Adverts had three 45s that year, so did The Clash – how great was 'Complete Control'? The Buzzcocks released the brilliant 'Spiral Scratch' e.p. and 'Orgasm Addict'. There was 'Neat, Neat, Neat' from The Damned, The Jam's 'In The City' calling card, 'God Save The Queen' by the Pistols…all strong contenders.

If I had to choose one song I'd go for 'Blitzkrieg Bop' by The Ramones, which was infectious, timeless and perfect.

So many records, so many gigs, so much talent, so much joy.

JOHN ROBB

Punk the cultural big bang that changed everything for some of us. It was a playground to chase your dreams and your desires. It was the perfect time to be 16 with a great sound track and unique myriad sense of styles that screamed 'do it yourself!'. So we did.

It was the lightning bolt that affected us as strongly growing up in Blackpool as it affected people in London. We were transfixed, inspired and thrilled.

It was a time when pop music was a high decibel freak show of Oxfam chic dandies dressed to thrill inspired by a Robin Hood style gang of vagabonds and flawed folk heroes that unleashed that big bang of energy that empowered us to make our own version of events. It was the only youth culture that had no rules, no codes. Everyone's idea of what it was is totally different and that's its strength.

It was our great escape and chance to make music, art, culture on our own terms and we didn't need anyone's permission to do it.

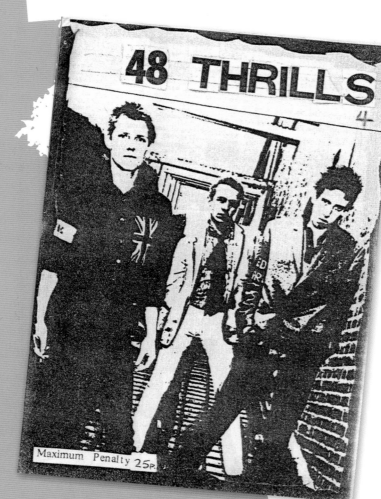

JON SAVAGE

The doubles often have it: 1933, 1944, 1955, 1966… But rarely has a year been so flagged up as 1977, the year when the two sevens clashed, a year of judgement as Culture's Joe Hill envisioned – when "past injustices would be avenged." Or, as Bo Jangles toasted on his version 'Prophesy Reveal', "this here 1977 nah go well dread. Cause you know Garvey's words must come true: all brutality and war must come to a half, war and trouble and fire are natty's fault. Equality and justice must stand, and all righteous men must stand too y'know."

As if in an echo, The Clash's vision of the year presented a youth and a nation on the point of explosion: "Knives in West 11/Ain't so lucky to be rich/Sten guns in Knightsbridge." They called for the destruction of previous icons – no Elvis, Beatles, Rolling Stones – at the same time as they counted down to the totalitarian nightmare of 1984. Superheated rhetoric to be sure, but there was always going to be something extraordinary about 1977: anyone with any pop culture antennae could feel it, something was going to blow.

Just like it is today, England was dreaming. The only people with the bravery, talent and sheer force to point this out were the Sex Pistols. The Jubilee Boat Trip was not a musical highpoint but a dramatic face-off between the country old and new. The forces of reaction won in the short term, but Punk won in history. To be involved with Punk in the summer of 1977 laid you open to hostility or worse – proper violence – and amid all the discussion that followed one thing has been forgotten: it was for the brave.

A sample playlist: Sex Pistols 'God Save The Queen'/Clash 'What's My Name'/Damned 'Neat Neat Neat'/Generation X 'Day By Day'/Bo Jangles 'Prophesy Reveal/Ramones 'Shock Treatment'/Saints 'This Perfect Day'/Adverts 'Quickstep'/Desperate Bicycles 'The Medium Was Tedium'/The Slits' What A Boring Life'/Junior Murvin 'Tedious Dub'/Buzzcocks 'Orgasm Addict'/Donna Summer 'I Feel Love'/David Bowie 'Moss Garden'/Glenroy Wilson 'Wicked Can't Run Away'/Wire 'Mr. Suit'/ Boys 'Soda Pressing'/Iggy Pop 'The Passenger'/Talking Heads 'No Compassion'.

A few memorable gigs: Heartbreakers, Roxy January/Damned, Roxy January/Adverts, Roxy February/Clash, Harlesden March/Iggy Pop, Aylesbury March/Sex Pistols and the Slits, Screen on the Green April/Buzzcocks and Wire, Roxy April/Blondie and Television, Hammersmith Odeon May/Subway Sect, Rainbow May/Ramones, Saints and Talking Heads, Roundhouse June/Last Night at the Electric Circus October/Siouxsie and the Banshees, The Music Machine November.

As winter set in, there was a sense of time running out. On 'Pink Flag', Wire worked on the numbers – "at least 17 plus three score, this is 77/Nearly heaven, it's black, white and pink" – while nailing the moment's frantic imperative: "Don't just watch, hours happen/Get in there kid and snap them." On the 31st the Ramones played the Rainbow Theatre – a fantastic show that was a summation of all they had achieved and, in retrospect, their high point. By the time everyone left the aftershow party, it was 1978. Things would be very different.

MARK P

(from a 1977 interview by Barry Cain))

I used to really believe that the kids would change something but they never will. They're naïve, they can't see the truth. Outside London especially, they're limited to reading the gutter press and I don't think you can ever break that media system. *International Times* tried to and failed. *Time Out* tried to, and now it's a conservative magazine.

It's just no use having alternatives.

Sniffin' Glue will never take over anything. The Clash can't go on for ever. I mean, what a contradiction – CBS demanding a release of 'Remote Control' as a single when that record is all about such manipulation. There's just no unity any more. How can I possibly relate to kids in Bradford who put safety-pins through their ears? And how can they possibly relate to me with the Zappa and Can influences? And if that's the case there's just no scene left. But I'm happy with that. I've lost the high I used to get back in September and October '76.

We meant something then. We knew who our audience was, people trusted us. But now I can't get enthusiastic about the scene. I like The Clash now in the same way I've liked any band over the last ten years. This is not the be-all and end-all. There will be other scenes. If my band don't relate to the Punks – I'm sorry, I apologise, but I'm never gonna change. If you're expecting Mark P to destroy, to clamour for anarchy and trip up all the MPs then you're gonna be disappointed. I'm not into that at all.

I got involved with the Step Forward label because It was a natural progression to being involved in actually making records. I simply wanted to put out records I liked. I didn't want to keep on writing about bands. That got to be a bit of a high horse. People didn't think I had the right to say a band was good or bad. In fact, I've just written my last piece for *Sniffin' Glue*.

The *Sniffin' Glue* office is next door to the Step Forward office. It has no electricity so a cable is fed out of the window along the ledge into our office.

I've had an idea for a band since last September. In fact, I actually had one – the New Beatles – a kind of anti-legend, but that never got past the rehearsal stage. So now I'm in Alternative TV. I can't play guitar so I play by a series of dots. I don't particularly want to learn how to play either. The concentration it would take to learn would spoil the on-stage experience, although I like things to be hard. I'm into Zappa and Can and jazz. I don't want to write songs for the people, I ain't a writer for the kids. But that doesn't mean I don't want people to be interested in us. I just want to get on stage and say something.

The only way I can do anything now is through music. If ten kids say they really liked what the band played and it helped them change their attitudes, then I'll be happy. We did this really long slow number down the Marquee last week, 'Alternatives To NATO', which has me reading a speech from an anarchist magazine. It got a great reaction and I'm convinced if you wanna change anything you've got to do it through music and music alone. I ain't a good enough writer to do it through writing.

I'm not interested in singles. I want to put out an album right away.

It's no use coming out with all the anarchy bit and throwing it in their faces, they'll take no notice. Win them with music. I want to go straight into the big venues and not piss around with the pub and small club circuit. That's a complete waste of time. I wanna play the Empire Pool.

I've never cared about getting a tight band. Alternative TV ain't tight and that's why it works.

If I want to do an instrumental break when I feel like it, I will and it's up to the others to follow me.

I haven't got old friends. I'm not one for a gathering of the clans. I was never involved in the gang thing. You play safe when you start relying on others. When most people leave school their brains ain't developed. They'll go to work in a factory and the most frightening thing is, a geezer will go there because his mate did. He's basing his whole career on something his mate did. So, then you get to thinking that the audience you're reaching is full of kids completely satisfied with their lot and that's why you can't preach anarchy to them. But I can give them music.

We need a spokesman for the whole scene. Johnny Rotten was, but he's slagged everyone off so much he ain't any more. And there's no way I'm a spokesman. But we do need someone.

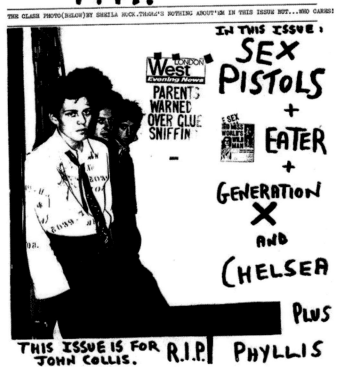

MICK O'SHEA

I was 14 when the Sex Pistols burst into the public consciousness following their teatime tête-à-tête with Bill Grundy on the *Today* show. *Today* was only broadcast within the London area, and as my dad favoured the *Daily Telegraph*, both the 'Filth' and the ensuing 'Fury', passed me by. The furore surrounding the release of 'God Save The Queen' would be the talk of the playground several months later, as we couldn't believe that a pop group would dare to call the queen a "moron" in her Silver Jubilee year.

As my interest in newspapers didn't extend beyond the back pages, I hadn't seen a photograph of the Pistols, and I simply imagined them to look no different than Status Quo, Led Zeppelin, or every other long-haired, denim-clad muso.

I had about as much interest in music as I did in the monarchy. In fact, I'd never so much as bought a single, let alone an album. I did, however, allow myself to get caught up with the banter as to what the names of Johnny Rotten and Sid Vicious' fellow Sex Pistols might be. The front-runners were Joe Strummer and Dee Generate, though I remember Burt Purple being a serious contender for a time. But there my interest in either The Pistols or Punk rock would probably have ended had it not been for the arrival at my school of a certain Kevin Grey.

Kev and his family had recently relocated to Accrington from their native Stockton-On-Tees in County Durham. As with any new kid in school, Kev was the focus of attention; even more so when he came bounding through the school gates sporting "bog-brush hair" and a safety-pin dangling from an earlobe. You can imagine the stick he got, and I have to confess that I initially joined in with the ridicule and piss-taking.

My Pistols epiphany came a few weeks later upon seeing the 'Pretty Vacant' promo video on *Top Of The Pops* (Thursday, 14 July 1977). Even now, four decades on, I can still remember the jolt on seeing them in the flesh as it were. It wasn't so much the music, even though Glen's ludicrously simple – yet instantly captivating – three-note intro still sets my spine a tingling. It was the Pistols' visual dynamic that grabbed me by the balls (never quite

DEE GENERATE

PUNK HITS

COULD YOU please give my address to Sandra Quick, the punk mum. I have a copy of **RECORD MIRROR** issue April 2 she can have. Being a punky mym myself I feel the same as her, and get spiteful remarks from

relinquishing its grip, either). From that point on I was only interested in talking about one thing: the Sex Pistols. I wanted to know everything about them and literally bombarded poor Kev with questions.

I started accompanying Kev and his small coterie of acolytes to various discos about town. They, like Kev, had customised their school uniforms in what became colloquially known as the "Jam look"; whilst adding varying accoutrements during after-school hours. One or two were even sporting bin-liners, no doubt having caught The Sun's "Top 10 tips on how to be a Punk." I felt like a total dick trying to master the pogo as I still had shoulder-length hair and was sporting flares. But no one ever held me to task. Punk was about attitude, after all.

My Mum and Dad were far from strict, but I knew there was sod all chance of my being allowed to put a safety-pin in my blazer, let alone get my hair spiked. They were totally unaware of my metamorphism . . . at least until I returned home one Saturday afternoon with a copy of *Never Mind The Bollocks*. I'd saved my pocket money and sold my prized Subbuteo stuff, but was still some way short of the £3.15 retail asking price. Mum, surprisingly, agreed to make up the shortfall when I told her I wanted to buy an album. I was equally surprised that she didn't think to enquire after the name of the artist, as my record collection up to that pivotal point in time consisted of a K-Tel Elvis LP, and a Subbuteo single that simulated crowd noise and inane ditties such as 'She'll Be Coming Round The Mountain', and 'Eee-aye-addio, We're Gonna Win The Cup'. The look on mum's face as she cast her eyes over *Bollocks'* artwork was indescribable.

Bollocks' supposedly offensive title led to a farcical court case and leading chain stores such as Woolworths, WH Smiths, and Boots refusing to stock the album. Many independent retail outlets were careful to keep the sleeve hidden from view ... away from 'innocent' eyes. This was certainly the case at the Disc and Tape Exchange where I'd purchased my copy (Accrington had three record shops, but this was the only one stocking the album). Such was our meagre info on The Pistols that my mates and I were eager to settle the argument once and for all as to who was in the Sex Pistols.

The confusion stemmed from the Jones/Matlock/Cook/Rotten song-writing credit featuring on the 'Anarchy In The UK', 'God Save The Queen', and 'Pretty Vacant' singles when Sid Vicious was

most definitely a Sex Pistol? The waters had been further muddied with the recent repeat screening of the Pistols performing 'Anarchy' live on *So It Goes*. It was a Sunday night and I remember being glued to the TV – all the while fervently praying that mum and dad wouldn't arrive home from their local to spoil the party and puzzling over why the fresh-faced guy playing bass on screen didn't look remotely anything like he did in the 'Pretty Vacant' video. Oh, the shame ...

My obsession with The Pistols was such (and it was an obsession), that several months would pass before I came to embrace The Clash, The Damned, Buzzcocks, and Generation X et al. But this was simply because I'd put the Pistols on such a high pedestal. Imagine my excitement on hearing that a date had been lined up at the

Mayflower in Manchester as part of a UK March tour. The fact that I was still only 15, and probably wouldn't have got through the Mayflower's door didn't enter my head. Indeed, the Mayflower date was all I could think of whilst pouring over the transatlantic communiqués (and accompanying photographs) in the music papers whilst The Pistols war-wagon rumbled across America on their debut US tour.

Then came the fateful day (Thursday, 19 January) when the news broke that the Pistols had split whilst in San Francisco. The weather was atrocious that day, with much of Britain blanketed in snow. I was late getting to school, and probably wouldn't have bothered making the effort had I not had a mock Geography exam that afternoon. As it turned out, I needn't have bothered because with half the staff failing to make it to school the mock exams were cancelled and we were all sent home.

I was beside myself at the news of the Pistols' split, and as absurd as it seems now. it was as though there'd been a death in the family. I was so distraught that I felt compelled to make some kind of statement, to nail my colours to The Pistols' mast in a show of solidarity. The following evening whilst Mum and Dad were enjoying their Friday night out, I took a pair of scissors to my hair, trembling with nervous excitement as each curly lock fell away and tumbled to the bathroom floor. Mum and Dad went absolutely berserk, but the deed was done.

The Sex Pistols had made their last tuneless racket (or so we thought), but my Punk rock adventure was only just beginning ...

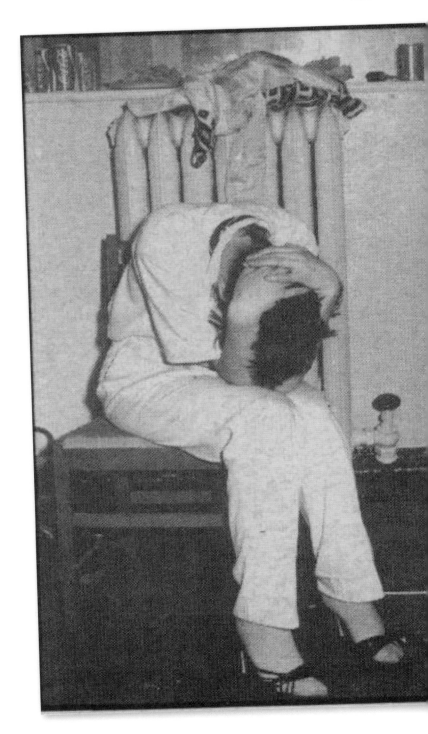

PAT GILBERT

It was the summer of '78. My bedroom door had a dartboard hung on the inside, to which I'd pinned a colour pull-out poster of Billy Idol from my sister's *Jackie* magazine.

I aimed a dart and – bang – Billy got one right in his bollocks! One hundred and eighty! Life was changing, in fact, from a boy into a teenager. I was 12-years-old and since the previous autumn I'd been growing very fond of this thing called Punk. There was only one Punk in our school, in the fifth year, who styled himself on Sid Vicious, and one evening he laid down in the road near our local bus stop and invited cars to run over him. Sadly, they didn't. But it was the music that got me.

The Jam's records spoke to me in a way I'd never experienced before. Their 19-year-old singer, Paul Weller, was a bolshie bastard, but he sang in a voice from the suburbs you knew was real. 'Away From The Numbers' made me feel… sad? Wistful? Complete? All those things, and also fiercely proud to be who I was, a kid alone in a crowd. Maybe for the first time I felt understood. (Thank you, Paul.) There was poetry there, definitely, something that went deep.

Then there was The Clash – my God! They looked like they'd stepped out of Punk rock war film, urban soldiers waging a guerrilla attack, with hard, sullen stares to match. 'White Riot', with the police siren on the single version, actually sounded like you were in a riot! 'White Man In Hammersmith Palais' was unlike anything I'd heard before, and sent an electric shock down your spine at the, "If Adolf Hitler flew in today" bit. The imagery, the lyrics – it was all an education, and so much more interesting than Geography classes at Cowplain Comprehensive School.

Never Mind The Bollocks was only fully digested shortly after The Pistols had split, but had a profound affect, though unlike The Jam and The Clash, I never fantasised about actually being in the group. 'Bodies', 'Holidays In The Sun' and 'New York' still make me want to smash things up; lord knows what they were doing to me at 12. Of course, I utterly devoured all that came in the wake of Punk's first wave – Siouxsie, Generation X (Derwood the guitarist was very cool), The Ruts, The Damned's Machine Gun Etiquette, The Undertones, SLF, Buzzcocks, TRB, Wire, PiL, The Slits, even the Boomtown Rats (but don't tell anyone). I was lucky to see several of those bands live when I was still at school.

Punk made me political and unafraid. It made me feel I wasn't alone. It helped make me the human being I am today. The sun was always shining back then.

Thank you, Punk Rock.

RICHARD CABUT

What was your introduction to Punk?

A Thrills piece by Neil Tennant in the *NME* describing the Sex Pistols Nashville pub contretemps of 23 April 1976. Wow, I thought, a band that beats up their own fans! I saw Dr Feelgood play in the same year – mid-set Captain Sensible crept up behind Lee Brilleaux and gave him a mighty two-handed shove into the audience. What a wag.

How did Punk infect your soul?

It fuelled my dreams of escape. I lived in small-town, working/lower-middle class suburbia – Dunstable, Bedfordshire, 30 miles from the capital. There, kids left school and went on the track, the production line, at the local factory, Vauxhall Motors. If you got some qualifications you could join the civil service. I didn't want either. Instead, I was in love with Punk Rock. I was in love with picking up momentum and hurling myself forward somewhere, anywhere. Rip up the pieces and see where they land.

Did you make friends through Punk?

Yes. Punk had the effect of, overnight, making all the school kingpins, the hard kids into football aggro, as well as the brainboxes with copies of Pink Floyd under their arms, irrelevant, out of step and laughable. Instead, the outsiders, those who had been previously scorned, found each other.

What did Punk mean to you?

Have you ever seen the old TV show *Bewitched?* In one episode, the character Endora, a witch, says of humans, "They all look the same to me, noses to the grindstone shoulders to the wheel, feet planted firmly on the ground, no wonder they can't fly!" She adds: "It's fine for them but not for us. We are quicksilver, a fleeting shadow, a distant sound that has no boundaries through which we can't pass. We are found in music, in a flash of colour, we live in the wind and in a sparkle of star..." which is kind of how I thought of Punk at that time.

It inspired me to create. I wrote my first fanzine, *Corrugated Boredom* (which later became *Kick*), pondering pretentiously on Dada and Surrealism, and penned bad poetry. I also bashed away on an old four-string acoustic guitar and wrote crappy, clichéd songs. I remember one: "Blades for flowers/drainpipes for jeans/hippies are dead/And they'll never return/ 67 reversed has destroyed that dream." Yeah. I went on to write for the *NME* (under the pen name Richard North) and various other publications. These days I write books and plays.

What were your hopes for it?

I thought it would change the world. I was positive that self-empowered, autodidactic, spiky guttersnipes were an upsurge of the future, certain to overcome the old social order.

What was your favourite Punk moment?

Flicking V-signs during the Jubilee itself, while nicking union flags from wherever they were to be found (everywhere), and invariably hanging out in the ladies (à la the Roxy Club) — although this had repercussions.

What did you think of Punk after 1977?

I liked the Punk scene in the early eighties. I liked it in the mid-seventies, too. The late seventies, though, were like the third Monday in January, officially recognized by the medical profession as the day on which more UK citizens wake up depressed than any other. The reality of another grinding year kicks in, the horror of the Christmas credit card bill bites, and the misery of another rain dashed day dawns. It was like that. But the early eighties was another Punk Spring. Punk at that time became a way of life for an increasingly large and motivated group of people. Moreover, folk were, to paraphrase Malcolm McLaren, creating an environment in which they could truthfully run wild. We were making scenes that took people away from the confines of school and work. Instead of just listening to records in isolation and going to the odd gig, people were having life adventures.

What did you read and listen too for your Punk fix?

In my bedroom, there was *Sniffin' Glue* and *Other*

Self Defence Habits (July '77), a bit of Sartre, *48 Thrills* (bought off Adrian at a Clash gig), Sandy Robertson's *White Stuff* (from Compendium in Camden) and John Peel, of course.

And tons of records – I loved the smell of fresh new Punk vinyl, as well as the slightly different scent of Jamaican imports (pressed on old recycled vinyl, because of cheapness rather than eco awareness) – all of it a shining, odorous promise of unexpected imaginings. It smelled of the future. Ah, the intensity of sitting in a loud room in a silent town, full of electricity. Floating above circumstances. Soaring…

Fave Punk song, album, act, concert?

On the way to a Clash gig, on January 25, 1978 Steve and I join a big group of new Punks, maybe 30 or 40 strong, walking along the main road. A police car stops us, and everyone waits for his or her turn to be searched. The kid in front of me surreptitiously pulls out a gun, a real revolver that he's nicked from a party, apparently, and passes it back through the group to a girl who sticks it in her handbag, crosses the road and walks away. I should have done the same. The gig itself is a bloodbath. Different estates slug it out with each other — Lewsey Farm v Stopsley — people stagger around with axe wounds, blood everywhere, the Wild West. A support band called the Lous gets killed, the Sex Pistols' minder English wanders around with a knife. I'm backstage and The Clash are worried: they're popping Mogadons (a downer). I'm worried, too – worried that I'll get stuck forever in all this bollocks. I know it's time to move, which, I do – to London. And, as it's obligatory to say in pieces like this, I'm still moving.

Fave item of clothing?

God Save the Queen T-shirt from Seditionaries.

How much did you spend on clothes and where did you buy/get them?

I was suburban Punk Everykid in pins and zips, with a splattering of Jackson Pollock and a little Seditionaries.

Favourite Punk music venues?

The California Ballroom – Dunstable's equivalent of the Lacy Lady or Global Village. Since '75 or so, hip kids had been travelling from miles around (even from London) for the plastic sandals and pegs scene there. It was all quite retro — forties swing fashions — until Punk.

Who were your Punk role models?

Patti Smith and Malcolm McLaren.

And villains?

The Boomtown Rats – they epitomised all the fakers and fuckers who quickly started to infest Punk.

How did it change you?

For the better. Or the worse. Depending on how you look at these things.

Did Punk achieve what you'd hoped for?

Yes, it quite plainly changed the world.

What was Punk's legacy?

Ideas. Ways of looking at the world. These days I still like the slogans associated with Punk. I like the poetry of that sort of politics. I once wrote a sort of verse, which talked about the Romance of Anarchy becoming Reality. I still believe that the romance is grounded in a reality that makes clear that, on all levels, the process of daily life is based on a trade of humiliations and aggro, as the Situationists said. I still think that 'alienated work is a scandal', that so-called 'leisure' is an affront, and that 'real life is elsewhere.' Where? Well, the pertinent questions, I still think, are not about restructuring economic systems, although I admit on a day-to-day level that helps, but about how quickly the underpinnings of society – all the givens, great unmentionables, so-called axioms – the fact that it is a closed-loop feedback system which easily sops up and throws back challenges and critiques – can be dissolved. I demand that this happens. And I feel, to paraphrase the Situ slogan and Malcolm McLaren's shirt, I am entirely reasonable in my demand for the impossible.

Did you fall in love while a Punk song was playing?

Love is two minutes and fifty seconds of squelching noises… wasn't it?

Did you date any members of Punk bands?

Yes. And I lived for seven years with one. We were still young. We were busy dreaming in Camden Town.

Were Punks more promiscuous than say mods, skinheads, hippies, soul boys etc?

I doubt it.

Did you wear overtly sexual clothes?

Not consciously.

Did you think the style made you look more attractive?

Absolutely. We strutted our Billy-the-Kid sense of cool — bombsite kids clambering out of the ruins — posing our way out of the surrounding dreariness. We were living in our own colourful movie (an earlyish Warhol flick we liked to think), which we were sure was incomparably richer, more spontaneous and far more magical than the depressing, collective black-and-white motion-less picture that the 9-5 conformists, or those that stumbled around with their booze-fuelled regrets, had to settle for.

What was the most romantic/sexiest Punk song?

'Anarchy in the UK'.

Did being a Punk prevent you from getting married and having a family? Or the opposite?

In Dunstable, Trevor and Nancy had been going out with each other since 3rd Form and watched telly round each other's house every night, not saying a word. I didn't know what I wanted, but I knew I didn't want any of that shit. (Now, I have a

EAT THE RICH

family with four kids)

Was Punk sexy?

Of course.

Did Punk merely perpetuate the hippy maxim of free love – were Punks hippies in disguise?

Well, rejection of the bourgeois ethos was part of the deal.

Did you have your first snog at a Punk gig? What was playing?

Wraparound shades were worn after dark so that everything was but murk, which might explain a heavy snogging session that turned out to be same-sex when I took the glasses off – rolling about on the stage while the Damned were playing. Divine decadence!

Who were the sexiest band?

The Velvet Underground – their archetype spoke of viciousness, lust 'n' hate and leather (a fantasy of style); life as film noir, existential, nihilistic and a little apocalyptic, I guess; silver art; white heat; pale, frail glamour; the sheen of squalor that spangles; downtown slow dive lowlifes; and other cheap throwaway thrills. You get the idea. It was bound to end in tears.

Pics. Me in 1977, and in early 80s - and with band I played in for a while - Brigandage (I'm on left, spiky hair).

ROSALIND RUSSELL

Punk, as a genre, seemed to me to be the hardcore of what was actually a much wider kick-back against bloated prog-rock. Although I'd class The Damned as Punk (and highly entertaining they were too), I wouldn't describe The Stranglers or The Jam as Punk; their songs were altogether more considered and commercial. Musically, Punk was pretty unstructured, the quality of playing questionable. But in fairness, the raw energy and ethic occasionally genuine.

I take issue with the Sex Pistols as pioneers of Punk, because they were as much a manufactured band as The Monkees or The Spice Girls. Manager Malcom McLaren had a tin ear, as far as I'm concerned, but he was an exemplary marketing man. I did (as far as I know) the last interview with Sid Vicious before he went to New York with Nancy, and was imprisoned for her murder. I might say here that I do not believe he killed her; he worshipped her, even while they were both heavily under the influence of the heroin they'd taken while I was with them. He told me Nancy was the first girl he had ever slept with.

Sid was obviously, even to me then, a young man with learning difficulties (and Nancy certainly wasn't the brightest button in the box). He was suggestible and a good fit for a sharp-eyed marketing man to set loose in an anarchic band which would garner massive publicity. He was good copy. At the end of that interview, I felt desperately sorry for him. His parting words to me were: "Please don't make me look stupid."

By and large, I disliked Punk, although I applaud the rocket it put up the record company behemoths like EMI. It was unmusical, testosterone-driven and frequently hostile (or maybe that last bit was just applied to female journalists).

I was sent by *Record Mirror* to cover the Pistols' gig on the boat on the Thames. The various cliques were squabbling amongst themselves, it was disorganised and very boring. When a few of the participants began to get more aggressive, I'd had enough. I went up to the captain on the bridge and told him a fight had broken out (an exaggeration, I admit). He immediately radioed the police, turned the boat around and headed back to the pier into the waiting arms of the constabulary. Hallelujah, free at last!

I leapt onto the jetty, legged it up Villiers Street to Charing Cross station, found a phone (this was before mobiles) and filed the copy. I got my story, McLaren got his headlines.

Cynical but true.

TONY PARSONS

What I remember most of all is the first time I encountered Punk.

It was a Punk festival at the 100 Club on Oxford Street in the summer of 1976. A friend and I had escaped from our night shift at Gordon's gin factory in Islington. We had bunked off looking for fun. I found more fun than I could handle. Fun that would change my life, and get me started as a writer.

I had heard wild rumours that rock music – for so long stale and middle-aged – had been returned to the youth. And when I walked down the steps of that old jazz club, I saw at once that it was true.

The music was crude, basic, no more than a handful of power chords played extremely loudly. It might have been The Damned on stage. But it was more exciting than anything I had ever seen.

I had grown up loving music but by the middle of 1976 it all felt old, self-indulgent and tired. Punk restored music to the young. It made music loud, brash and exciting again – everything it had been when Elvis was young and thin and tearing it up. Punk made music seem within reach. I met a number of fledgling musicians that night – Punk always had a strong sense of community – and they just seemed like everyone I grew up with. I had never met them before. But I recognized them.

I remember the atmosphere in the 100 Club was quite wild – glasses were thrown, tough poses were struck. It was more like a football match than a concert. If anything, that made me love it all the more.

In 1976, the world told the young that they should settle down to boring, unexceptional lives of no meaning.

And Punk told the world it was wrong.

VIVIEN GOLDMAN

Punk brought me a community of musical girls, which had definitely not existed before – in London, the Slits, the Raincoats, the Delta 5, the Mo-Dettes… in New York, ESG and the Bush Tetras. Knocking about with them all was very strengthening and definitely helped free me to make my own music. I was working on a rock weekly when Punk began in London, and most of my colleagues did not want to see their lads' own rock biz construct change.

But thanks to the recklessly freewheeling, inclusionary spirit of Punk, it did.

So, Punk was a big step in an ongoing process of offbeat artists making their own indie way into the marketplace – and of women finding and defining their sound, style and careers with more agency than ever before.

CAREER OPPORTUNITIES...

The Photographers...

DEREK D'SOUZA

The closest I ever got to seeing The Sex Pistols....

It was the summer of 1978, an exciting time for music, it was the changing of the guard, with Punk and new wave music having exploded onto an unsuspecting Britain. The changes were reflected not only in the music scene, but also the fashion. While I was never a Punk, (ripped up clothing, safety pins and bondage gear never appealed to me), the music was so exciting and like nothing I had ever heard before! At the tender age of 19, I was drawn to the City and the Music, and it was great to be going to gigs where both band and audience were of a similar age.

Strangely enough it was a slightly older group, the Steve Gibbons Band, that I'd decided to go and see, and dragged my younger cousin Darryl (he was 18) along for company.

The date was Monday, 7 August 1978, the venue the Music Machine in Camden. In those days, you either went along to the box office and bought your ticket in advance or paid on the door.

It was in retrospect a great line up, although I hadn't heard of the supporting bands at the time: Steve Gibbons Band, The Slits, Autographs, John Cooper Clarke.

I have two very distinct memories from the gig. Firstly, during The Slits set for some reason Ari Up decided to pull down her ski pants and take a pee on the stage – not something you see every day! Anyway, a great set by The Slits.

Secondly, when I stood on the steps watching the gig, Sid Vicious accidentally trod on my foot and I spilled my beer. He was very apologetic and very polite, not at all how I thought he would be.

All in all a great night and worth the hassle of getting home late and struggling to keep awake the next day at work, and that brief encounter was the closest I ever got to seeing The Pistols...

FRANCESCO MELLINA

Liverpool, 1977. I'd heard on the grapevine about this club called Eric's. I was told there were some strange people frequenting the place. I decided that it was worth seeing what was going on.

One evening I arrived there carrying my camera and feeling quite excited about going in. The room was dark, hot and sweaty. Strangely, I felt at home instantly, a feeling that I belonged there. My evening was made remarkable as I was told that the band playing that night were The Ramones. How lucky was that? My first visit in Eric's and The Ramones were playing! I photographed the band that night during their stunning set and that was my introduction to PUNK!!

JILL FURMANOVSKY

I was never a Punk myself but I admired their work ethic – if you can play three chords you can form a band. I had trained for two weeks and become a photographer. That was the mood of the time and it suited me.

I was 23 years old in 1976 and had done my growing up, music wise, to the hippy generation. Indeed Pink Floyd were one of my main clients then. So, when the Sex Pistols thrust their disrespectful faces into our shocked ones via the Grundy show on TV, nothing was ever the same again. I was at The Ramones gig at the Roundhouse in the summer of 1976 when they supported the Flaming Groovies, whom I'd photographed in the British Museum for *Sounds* earlier that day. The Ramones wiped the floor with the headliners. The audience looked like typical hippy-type students at that gig, but a year later when the Ramones headlined the same venue, the audience were wall to wall Punks.

In 1976, I met Mark P writer and editor of *Sniffin' Glue* and his mate Harry Murlowski who took pictures. They were at a Generation X gig at the Central London Polytechnic. A small scruffy girl stood mesmerised at the front watching Billy Idol. It was Ari Up (later of the Slits). She had come to the gig with her mum Nora, later to become John Lydon's partner. I introduced Harry and Mark to manager and agent Miles Copeland. They broke into an empty office next door to his in Dryden Chambers off Oxford Street. I saw the Queen drive by the mews for her Silver Jubilee. Harry ran a cable from Miles' office into theirs and that become *Sniffin' Glue's* headquarters. Malcolm McLaren was upstairs and The Pistols came and went followed by film crews waiting for the band to commit another outrage.

I helped Harry to print his pictures in my darkroom and I took a few myself for the *Glue*, but not of the Pistols. I photographed The Buzzcocks, The Clash, The Jam, The Stranglers, Slaughter and The Dogs, Siouxsie and The Banshees, Sham 69, Menace, The Adverts, and Chrissie Hynde who was wandering about the 100 Club looking for musicians to form her own band. Wayne County, Johnny Thunders, Blondie and Iggy were around – the second wave of Punks from America. I went to the Roxy Club and met Don Letts the DJ who introduced reggae to the Punks 'cos there weren't enough Punk records to play of an evening. I went to small pubs and clubs like Dingwalls and The Marquee. I saw the third wave of Punk, Squeeze, Elvis Costello, The Police, Devo, Talking Heads – they were all influenced by Punk.

Punk was a musical tsunami. By mid-79 it was all over and we were into the New Wave.

MARTYN GODDARD

My photographic career kicked off working in the music business by complete luck due to the enthusiasm for my work by a part-time lecturer at my art school. In 1974, he introduced me to Gered Mankowitz, rock snapper to the likes of the Rolling Stones and Jimi Hendrix. It was an amazing time for British rock music and within three years I had become established working with bands such as Queen and AC/DC before becoming immersed in the new wave and Punk revolution working with and producing album covers for The Jam, The Cure, Sham 69 and of course Blondie who had come to prominence in the UK.

At the beginning of my career, I photographed Ian Dury, who I think of as a sort of godfather of Punk, at the Victoria Palace when his band Kilburn and the High Roads were the support act for Sha Na Na. He was a charismatic front man even if the rest of the band were a bit wayward. Six years later, the *Telegraph Sunday Magazine* asked me to shoot a profile of Mr Dury who was now top of the pops.

Our first session was in Putney where I met the PR from Stiff Records, Magenta Divine, who was nothing if not stylish. It started to rain and things looked bleak until Ian arrived in a green Ford Cortina and shouted, "Where do you want to take the snaps?" or words to that effect. The rain was heavy by now but deep in the boot of my car I had an old golf umbrella that was colourful and large. It saved the day and we walked along the Thames river walk shooting at will and producing an interesting set of images to start the profile.

Home shoots were popular with the magazine editor but not with Ian Dury, so my next set of images were taken at a studio recording session in deepest Harlesden. Being keen, I turned up on time and on arrival two things were made clear, no flash photography and yes, Ian hadn't arrived yet. The place was dimly lit with fluorescent tubes and the odd spotlight so any hope of colour photography was out. I chose my good old standby, black and white Tri X film rated at 800 ASA, which would produce documentary style grainy prints. I settled down reading old copies of *NME* and studio recording trade magazines for a while until my subject turned up. A quick hello then into the studio until early afternoon and yes, we could shoot while the band took a break.

1977 was an amazing year for music and I was lucky to be around in the right place at the right time. I had produced the photographs for The Jam's *In The City* album and a series of single covers working with art director Bill Smith. The then Polydor creative director, Jo Mirowski, had another band lined up for my camera, Sham 69. I went to meet front man Jimmy Pursey at a greyhound kennel in Surrey as he reckoned on the place being a good location for shooting the single cover for 'Borstal Breakout'. Indeed, it was a great location – giant wooden doors which I had the band making their escape from, high walls topped with barbed which the band scaled, all shot in moody b&w to great effect. This was a Punk band with attitude, so we let Mr Pursey direct and I shot at a pace not letting the band have too much time to think. I just shot a lot of film quickly wanting to catch the action. To wrap up what was a great session, the four band members squeezed onto a settee in the kennel maids' hut, dartboard on the back wall and lit as if they were watching an old TV set.

The single sleeve was only just designed when the record company asked me to shoot an album cover and Jimmy once again was well involved with the shoot at an old-school building. The band had issues with their education and the *Tell Us The Truth* cover involved lots of finger pointing and carving graffiti into an old-school desk which we'd found in a junk shop. Jo's album cover and the single worked their magic.

Later I met up with Jimmy Pursey when he asked me to shoot the 'Hersham Boys' cover. Typical Jimmy in that we all met at a street sign in Hersham close to his home and he just rounded up friends, family and passers-by to pack my viewfinder, the only proviso was that we needed to see the street sign. Fun shot from a fun shoot.

In 1978, Toyah (Wilcox) and her band came through my Church Street Kensington studio doors. She had spade loads of attitude and had just become part of the art cinema scene after playing a part in a Derek Jarman film. This was one group that ideas flooded out of and Toyah would arrive with bags of props, which on one shoot included cobweb spray and a 12- inch dagger that I was not sure if Safari Records press office would take to. At another the studio session, she instructed the band to strip down to their underpants. Happy days.

In late June 1978, I found myself in the Record Plant studios in New York City with Blondie. They were in the studio recording their third album, *Parallel Lines*. This was my second visit to photograph the band as a month earlier I'd taken a £99 Freddie Laker DC10 flight to spend a week with them staying in the Gramercy Park hotel shooting Debbie Harry which became a cover story for the *Telegraph Sunday Magazine*. I had travelled with the group to Philadelphia when they were the support band for Alice Cooper and enjoyed photographing the band's one off gig at the Palladium in New York.

When I arrived at the studio for the first photo session for their record company Chrysalis, one of several planned for the week, I could sense a tense atmosphere. As a photographer, shooting in recording studios was always a problem on a technical level with period camera equipment and film stock in what were very dark functional spaces. Additionally, one had to work around the process of recording a record. It was soon evident that Blondie and Debbie Harry in particular. were having issues with record producer Mike Chapman. The group's New York Punk heritage was finding Chapman's quest for West Coast perfection overbearing. While I shot the images on contact sheet R427E (the negatives now lost), Debbie would have to sing short vocal passages which were overdubbed time after time, hence the various facial expressions she was making to the camera! Stiflingly boring in production for all members of the band, the album was to take just six weeks to record. Despite the record companies doubts about the album, it produced hit singles and reached number six in the US Billboard chart and number 1 in the UK album chart. The rest is history.

In August 1978, in association with Chrysalis

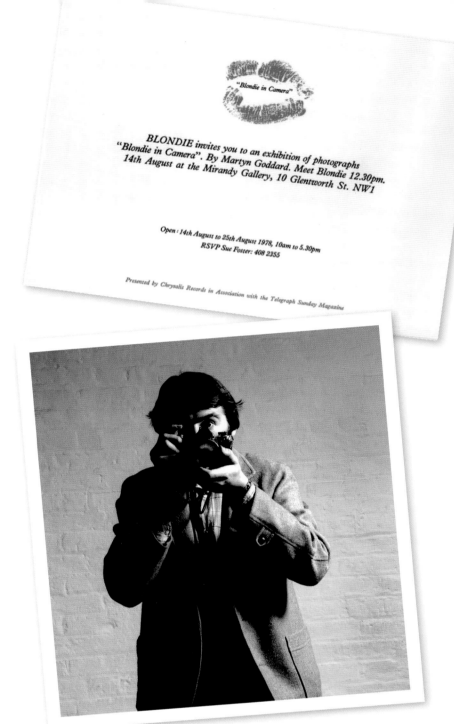

Records and the *Telegraph Sunday Magazine*, I staged the exhibition 'Blondie In Camera' at the Mirandy Gallery in Glentworth Street, London. It was a collection of the images from the two shoots in New York that year. The exhibition opening was to be the media launch of the latest single 'Picture This' and the presentation of a silver disc for the *Plastic Letters* album. So, at 2.30 pm August 14, the band arrived making their way through the crowded street full of fans who had been waiting all that morning. I certainly enjoyed the event which was given serious media coverage and we were able to sell signed prints for the band's favourite charity supporting diabetes research. I still have three prints but over the two weeks of the exhibition, three life size cut outs of Debbie Harry and the white label *Kissed* LP that I used for the *Parallel Lines* picture disc shot, all went AWOL.

VIRGINIA TURBETT

I'd love to say I was there at all those early Pistols and Clash gigs in '76 but I wasn't. I was going to a great many gigs since my early teens but I'd not got punk until half way into 1977.

My musical tastes were catholic: Bowie obviously, Lou Reed, Velvets, Iggy, Alex Harvey, Roxy Music, Beefheart, Traffic, Doors, King Crimson, Queen and, I reluctantly admit, even rocked down the front of a couple of gigs to Lynyrd Skynyrd in the mid-seventies.

Rock music had always been essential in my life. As a young teen, I lived for Thursday mornings when NME came out and, having read the gig guide, travelled miles to be at the front of the queue for tickets.

Early '77 and the red top papers were beginning to run the 'What's the world coming to?' headlines. Spiky-haired girls wore nothing but bin bags and ripped fishnets and swore proudly and loudly. People pierced their cheeks with babies' nappy pins and razor blades were worn as jewellery. This could be worse than the teds, the mods or the hippies – "Lock up your daughters!"

Hard to imagine now the hysteria created in the press around a group of very young people who were just doing what we, as parents and grandparents, now encourage our young to do – grow up, experiment, push boundaries, maximise creativity and not let anyone tell you what you can and cannot do.

I was living in Guildford in 1977 when a friend came back from Los Angeles having been part of the inception of *Slash* magazine. He was their UK correspondent and I was to become the photographer. I had a punk name but not a good one. That I'd never taken a photo didn't matter; this was punk and anyone could do anything if they wanted. That was the new order of things – breaking down all the rules, regulations and the hierarchy. Just get up, get out and go for it.

My introduction to punk was powerful and historically profound. I knew the Sex Pistols by reputation and not much else and I didn't know how to take photos. A crash course on my

boyfriend's Mamiya camera the night before was almost all I needed to get me through my first ever assignment – the Sex Pistols making the 'Pretty Vacant' video in TV Eye Studios in London!!!!! I had to go to a camera shop on Tottenham Court Road to ask how to change the film midway through the session.

The video shoot was followed by pints and kebabs at a pub in Whitfield Street with John, Sid, Paul and Steve, and then a trip to Seditionaries to buy a God Save The Queen T shirt. Peak Punk. It was one of those days that changed the course of the rest of my life and every time I see the 'Pretty Vacant' video, it sends a big shiver down my spine. My life wasn't the same after that and neither was my record collection.

In '76-77, there was a transition taking place amongst the youth of Britain. People went to a gig one night with long hair and flares and next day had all the hair off or spiked with gel, and trouser legs were tapered down calves and ankles with not an inch to spare. At gigs, new wave was becoming dominant and I witnessed this while watching X play the Troubadour's first ever punk gig in Los Angeles in 1977 when Exene started up an authentic bar-room brawl between the punks and Tom Waits and his entourage. "Don't fuck wi my fwends," said Waits as Exene berated the old hippies sitting at Waits' table in front of the stage.

We don't have the tribes and their music now; the listening of the young and old is eclectic. But back then, what you listened to was defined by what you were; a skin, a mod, a ted, a Punk, or a hippy. There was violence outside and inside the venues – sometimes it was really scary and dangerous getting in and out of a gig.

I remember leaving the Roundhouse after one of their Sunday afternoon mega gigs and running down Chalk Farm tube station and on to the tube tracks because we were being chased by skinheads. Another time, at a Rock Against Racism gig in Acklam Hall, we barricaded ourselves in the toilets as skinheads broke the windows with iron bars and beat up everyone who escaped the venue. I got punched in the head in the orchestra pit at Sham's Last Stand at the

Rainbow as the gig got taken over, and stopped, by over 100 National Front supporters, much to Jimmy Pursey's great distress. I had a punk friend wearing Vivienne Westwood bondage trousers and fearing for his life at a mod gig in the Marquee when the mods started picking out punks in the crowd for a beating.

For a while, it felt like fights broke out in the crowd at every gig in London. The Rut's 'Staring at The Rude Boys' illustrates this brilliantly and accurately: "The lights come alive in a blinding flash/Dance floor clears as the victims clash/Everyone leaves when the heavies arrive/Someone hits the floor, someone takes a dive."

Johnny Rotten told us in our *Slash* interview, "It's political to decide which can of baked beans you want nowadays," and he was right. Politics is entrenched in everything around us, so it was inevitable that punk and politics would become bedfellows. The Rock Against Racism and Anti-Nazi League gigs happened because lots of bands wanted to make a statement about what was happening in the country and define themselves as against the National Front and British Movement's presence at gigs. Punks came out in force to support anti-racism, to promote equality and to sing "Glad to be Gay" along with Tom Robinson. A punk gig often felt like a

place of education, with poetry – John Cooper Clarke, Attila the Stockbroker and Lynton Qwesi Johnson - and reggae and dub playing before and between bands that we'd later try to find at our local indie record shops.

The women and their bands who made and came from punk were inspiring and are still emulated today. Patti Smith, The Runaways, Siouxsie who's hair I tried, and failed, to copy, the Slits – bonkers and brilliant, Poly Styrene and X-Ray Spex (the second band I ever photographed), Gaye Advert singing 'Gary Gilmore's Eyes', Pauline Murray who had a striking and beautiful voice, Chrissie Hynde obviously, later the Modettes, who looked and sounded fantastic, and more. Women could get up on stage and not have to look like they'd spent hours blow drying their hair. They could (or couldn't but it didn't matter) play instruments. They could show their knickers in a way that definitely wasn't sexy and be as loud and brash as any man.

For *Sounds*, I travelled around the country photographing not only the bands with big local followings that hadn't been heard of in London, but also the local punks. I loved that everyone could embrace and work in the new culture; designing one-off clothes, making a single, writing a fanzine, starting a band. You could be anything you liked and if you waited outside Broadcasting House at 8 o'clock at night, you stood a good chance of catching John Peel on his way in and getting your music played that night to millions. It was accessible to the people – the very antithesis of the pomp and ceremony of rock that had preceded it.

It's impossible to talk about punk gigs without mentioning the gob. There was so much gob. It was really, really horrible. Some bands got it worse than others and being down the front trying to photograph The Clash or The Damned was particularly gruesome. I'd get it in my hair, all down my back, all over my cameras and lenses. Not all things punk were great – but I do feel very lucky that I was there at that time photographing the bands and the fans. It felt like an extraordinary time and that people still want to see the images I took 40 years ago is testament to this.

Punk had started in New York in 1974 with The Ramones, Patti Smith and Television. I had seen that the essence of punk could even survive on the U.S. west coast in places like the Masque club in Los Angeles with bands like The Zeros and The Weirdos, Black Randy, The Screamers and X. But it was never going to work in the spiritual home of the Grateful Dead and it didn't. I was present at what has been called "the night punk died" – San Francisco's Winterland where the Pistols moaned and groaned their way through what was to be their last ever gig. It was awful.

Inevitably, punk got embraced by mainstream culture. By the time Elizabeth Hurley wore her tabloid front cover safety pin dress, the real punk movement had evolved and moved on far from simplistic fashion statements. I love it that, 40 years on, there are young and old still sporting Mohicans, bondage trousers and writing slogans all over their clothes and that I hear music that sounds like it could have come out of Rough Trade in 1977.

It's a credit to the power of punk that there are new bands making music that's just as energetic and profound and that many of the original bands are still on the road and that we're all talking about it now, decades later.

Because it is still relevant to who we are.

new wave

NEWS

NAVIAN...

EXCLUSIVE PIX

...VOLT INTO
...TERITY

...D PURE
...ANIA
...with
...ulie
...urchill

ANOTHER
ROTTEN
POSTE...
INSID...

...E JAM...THE BOYS...THE ADVERTS...999...GENERATION X...THE HEARTBREAKE...

EVER FALLEN IN LOVE WITH SOMEONE...

The Fans...

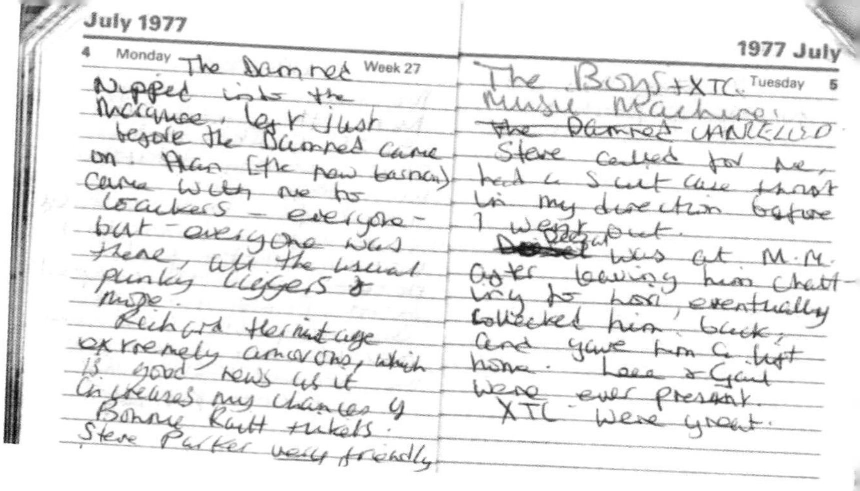

Handwritten diary entries:

> **4 Monday — The Damned**
> Nipped into the Marquee, left just before the Damned came on. Alan (the new bassist) came with me to Louises — everyone was there, all the usual punky liggers & ... Richard Hermitage extremely amorous, which is good news as it increases my chances of Bonny Rait tickets. Steve Parker very friendly.

> **5 Tuesday — The Boys + XTC**
> Music Machine. The Damned CANCELLED. Steve called for me, had a suit case thrown in my direction before I went out. ... was at M.M. after leaving him chatting to Lou, eventually collected him back and gave him a lift home. Lou + Gail were ever present. XTC were great.

AMANDA AUSTIN

Amanda, from Golders Green, was a regular at Punk gigs and ligs between '76-'78. She met Bob Geldof at one party and had a brief relationship with him. Luckily, she kept a diary…

The reason I didn't get too personal in my diaries was because my mum used to go through everything! I lived near Golders Green back then. In 1975, I worked as secretary to the editor of *Health and Efficiency* magazine published by Plant News. While there, our receptionist, Brigid, blagged some passes for *Old Grey Whistle Test* and Rory Gallagher was playing. I got to know the producer Mike Appleton and it just snowballed from there.

Two years later, when I was 19, I started going out with Jimmy Bain who was the bassist with bands like Rainbow and Dio and was playing with John Cale at the time. I couldn't arrange anything with him coz he was usually too out of it. I just thought people then were either stoned or drunk and I didn't know about other drugs and their effects. I just knew where to find Jimmy and that was that. Besides, he couldn't run away if he wanted to, he was too zonked. He used to crash out on my shoulder down the Speakeasy where he bought me champagne on my birthday. Thin Lizzy guitarist Brian Robertson, who formed the band Wild Horses with Jimmy, used to live with Jimmy in Pimlico. Back then people didn't really arrange to meet. You just knew where they'd be. There was no actual dating scenario. Put it this way, I didn't expect to be walked down the aisle.

20 June 1977 – Started work at Bronze record company as a typist.

4 July – Saw The Damned at the Marquee then went on to the opening of Vortex. I'd sorted getting The Heartbreakers for the opening night and I was the first name on the guest list. To this day I regret not asking for a copy,

15 July met Fachtna O'Kelly, the Boomtown Rats' manager, and he gave me a Boomtown Rats badge and invited me to a playback of the new Thin Lizzy album at the Roundhouse Studios

18 July – Went to the playback and met Bob Geldof. First time I saw Rats was at the Music Machine on 30 June. My mate Debbie was mad on him and I rung her to tell her he was there. After the playback, I went to The Roebuck pub before going on to a party at Country Cousins where Bob was being very attentive. I also met Shane McGowan at another party in Overend Watts' house in Acton. Shane was eating raw frozen peas direct from the freezer!

21 July – John Miller organised a tug-of-war in Hyde Park. Alex Harvey was there along with loads of bands. I met Bruce Brody, who became the keyboardist for Patti Smith and Tom Verlaine, and we went out for a while.

29 July – Went to the Marquee where I met Bob again. I said I had to pop next door for a while and Bob said he'd wait for me and when I got back 30 minutes later he was still waiting in exactly the same spot. He was being pursued by loads off other women at the time but he only had eyes for me. He once said to me that the words on my tombstone should be, 'She ligged her way through life.' An 'Ace Ligger' jacket was given to me by Thin Lizzy after I once ironed their stage gear.

Around this time I went out with Warren Cann from Ultravox a few times after meeting him at the Rainbow but he wasn't really my type.

7 September – I went to Dave Vanian's wedding

14 Sept – The Rats played the Marquee and Bob invited me for dinner to celebrate the band's second birthday party.

25 October – I went to the *Old Grey Whistle Test* with Bob to see The Runaways. Bob was doing the old courting dance – puffing out chest etc. to attract the glances of females – that was Bob.

He was still trying it on with me but I hadn't succumbed.

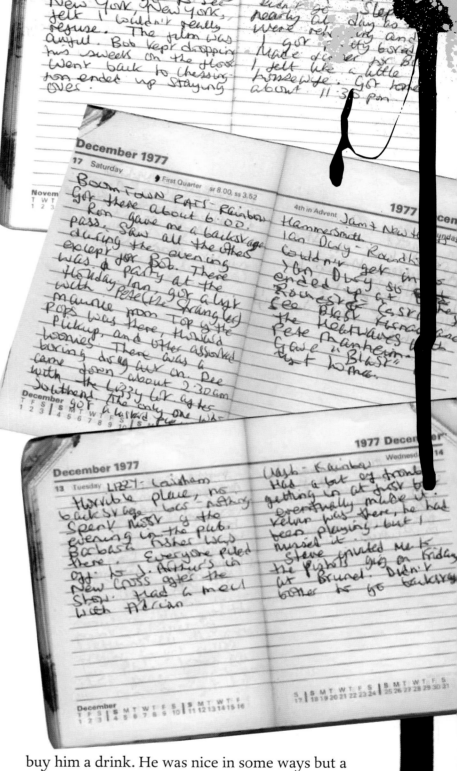

31 Oct - It was the official Rats second birthday party in a Fulham restaurant. Bob invited me but we didn't talk coz I got absolutely pissed. I was working at the Cowbell agency then.

9 November - Bob rang and asked me to go and see the movie *New York New York* at the Marble Arch Odeon. After the film, he offered to drive me home in his little grey car. He filled up with petrol at a petrol station in Park Lane and started driving south. I told him I lived in the opposite direction but he said he lived in this direction. He was staying in Chessington at the time where the Rats were rehearsing. When we got there, he asked me to make him dinner and I told him, 'It's your house, you make it.' My mum didn't know where I was. I stayed over that night. I succumbed…

11 Nov - He had a meeting in town and I met him there. He'd been wearing the same clothes for three days. I remember his T shirt – it had a picture of a strawberry with the word 'pop' on it. I thought, this isn't the man for me.

He wanted someone to chase him like Paula Yates eventually did. She pursued him relentlessly. I was relieved, she was like a stalker when it came to Bob. We kept in touch but we just weren't compatible.

25th November – Bob and I were at The Roundhouse and this woman was chasing him and I had a row at the bar with him.

Went to *TOTP* with him and he didn't want me to

buy him a drink. He was nice in some ways but a bit chauvinistic in others.

7th Feb 1978 - I saw Tom Robinson at a *Sight and Sound* in concert. I was obsessed with him and convinced myself I could turn him straight.

6th October – I was selling merchandise at Liverpool Empire and met Ali McMordie of Stiff Little Fingers who were supporting Tom Robinson. We were standing side-stage watching Tom Robinson play. He ended up becoming my first true love (on my part it was) even though it only lasted four months in 1978.

BOBBY PARRY

We all loved just growing up,
to the sound of PUNK,
U.S.A when just a pup,
I danced and I got drunk.
1970's, the Punk domain,
United Kingdom first,
Bowie as Aladdin Sane,
I had to quench my thirst.
Bobby Rotten I became,
and then I was so vain,
Johnny was the man to blame,
The Pistols born again.
It was known as Garage Rock,
later Proto Punk,
Tartan trousers waves of shock,
glue to feel defunct?
Punk Rock bands were at the top,
hard edged melodies,
singing styles to outdo Pop,
the lyrics they did freeze.
A time for me at just a teen,
The Beatles were my band,
all the sights that I had seen,
my wish for Punks to stand.
The Jam for me were different class,
But were they Punks or Mods?
'New Wave' is a term I'd pass,
because they were just Gods.
The New York Dolls & The Ramones,
ticking every box,
spearheaded angry tones,
you should have seen their frocks?
The Damned would damn old London Town,
The Clash would make some noise,
Sid was Vicious he would frown,
along with box of toys.
Stripey Mohair Uniform,
safety pins & chains,
this crew bred to none conform,
the trials & all the pains.
Toby Light & cans of Harp,
Mascara set the scene,
studs in noses very sharp,
but to us serene.
Joy Division were in sync,
Public Image scarred,
Fingers stiff, a little pink,
The Fall were acting hard.
Chelsea held a Magazine,
Abrasive Wheels would turn,

Sub humans were always seen,
the cities they would burn.
Railway stations, down the tube,
The Ruts would strut their stuff,
Discharge with some super lube,
X-Ray Spex were rough.
UK Subs, The Only Ones,
Cockney Rejects great,
hand in hand with 'All Mod Cons',
my destiny my fate.
999, The Partisans,
Vibrators, Ad Nauseam,
Wire, The Exploited clans,
The Slits a winning team.
The Anti Nowhere League, The Skids,
The Drones were soaring high,
A Red Alert for us Punk Kids,
with Gold-blade in the sky.
Angelic Upstarts, in Conflict,
The Lurkers hung around,
Ian Dury rhythm sticked,
The Cure was surely found.
The Rings did Blitz with solitude,
The Pogues they would Demob,
A Deadmans Shadow was so rude,
A One Way System job.
Dennis Menace, Argy Bargy, Chaos UK reigned,
Fire Exit with some Snuff,
The Toy Dolls never waned.
Charged GBH a Motley Crew,
Adam & The Ants,
take a bow in my review,
this poem is utter pants.
The sweaty throng of teenage kicks,
the vomit on the wall,
a tube of glue would surely fix,
the statues in the hall?
Cans of gas to get a buzz,
high on pure propane,
fighting with the fucking fuzz,
their loss to us a gain.
The Buzzcocks buzzed to keep in line,
The Undertones were right,
we all love Sham 69,
all part of the Punk Might!
In the City, Modern World,
would become a smash,
London Calling, Punks unfurled,
a banner for The Clash.
Blondie set the world on fire,

Hazel in a whirl,
Punks we sang just like a choir,
the wisdom in my pearl.
I was barely ten years old,
Showaddywaddy blues,
always roasting never cold,
a 'Ted Dance' in my shoes.
1977 came, to me it was unreal,
a Jubilee and river cruise,
The Pistols they did steal.
The pompous glory from Our Liz,
renditions lost in verse,
I then thought that, "They're the biz",
a kid who found a curse.
The older lads just freaked me out,
with kettles for handbags?
The rag & bone-man gave a shout,
of ,,,,, "Where's my effin rags?
The rags of course were on my arse,
me Ma well she did scream,
my Rollers days replaced with farce,
this era was my dream.
David Bowie was immense,
The Stranglers set me free,
The Captain wasn't making sense,
and Siouxsie was Banshee.
Doctor Feelgood wasn't well,
Lena Lovich sang,
'Money' was a living hell,
with riots and 'back-slang'.
Social decay Tory rule,
tore the land apart,
Maggie was the biggest fool,
but me I'd say,,,,, "A Fart".
Mods on Scooters were like mates,
sharing all the vibes,
sweaty concert replicates,
the force of these Two Tribes.
I was now an 80's teen,
The Jam & Clash still ruled,
I was part of the Punk Scene,
my tastes were never fooled.
Now I'm old and baldy too,
glasses like jam jars,
just about to see my view,
in dank & sweaty bars.
But I'm happy with my lot, j
just keeping things alive,
what I gave is what I got,
to see bands playing live.

All the classics from my past,
my attic full of dreams,
the notion that this book will last,
forever at the seams.
Nicky was a Punk yanno?
I have seen the pics,
showing lots of 'to & fro',
showing us her tricks.
Went full circle as a Mod,
her heart was not in two,
Punk & Mod became her God,
she done this all for you!
'Growing Up with Punk' is great,
a book of expertise,
written by my best 'Jam Mate',
great reading it will please.
An exhibition she will show,
that Punks are still a force,
she takes a chance and I just know,,,,,
there'll never be remorse!!!

BRYAN BIGGS

Punk and other junk shop reflections...

Punk started for me in 1974 when Deaf School formed at Liverpool Art College where I was studying fine art. Musically shambolic, dressed in charity shop clothes, and adopting daft names, they wanted to revolutionise pop.

At the city's alternative music epicentre, Eric's, its owner Roger Eagle had a plan. Punk came along at the right time to help him realise it. The club's soundtrack was extremely heavy dub, fifties/sixties r&b, a smattering of psych, rock'n'roll and wild jazz. The live acts: some of the aforementioned, but principally nutty new wave combos, playing there one week, on the cover of *NME* the next.

People eulogise about The Clash's visits, but the Tom Robinson Band was just as electric. X Ray Spex, XTC, The Pop Group, Dillinger, The Cramps, all more compelling and strange.

Even then, in 1977, you could see Strummer & Co adopting the rockist trappings that were the antithesis of Punk's founding spirit – to confound conformity, fuck about with genres, have a laugh and maybe produce something profound. The Table, The Prefects, Television Personalities, The Slits, Ed Sirrs' 'I think I think too much' – infinitely preferable to identikit Punk.

After a couple of problematic Eric's gigs – The Damned's pantomime Punk, complete with mini-riot of thrown chairs and Rat admitting his admiration for Jeff Beck, and ATV's nihilistic but totally endearing tirade against an uncaring audience – the floodgates were wide open for local bands to soar on Punk's cheeky promise: Big in Japan, Those Naughty Lumps, Teardrop Explodes, Moderates, Accelerators, The Pale Fountains, The Room, Lotus Eaters, It's Immaterial, Half Man Half Biscuit. Thanks Malcolm & Johnny.

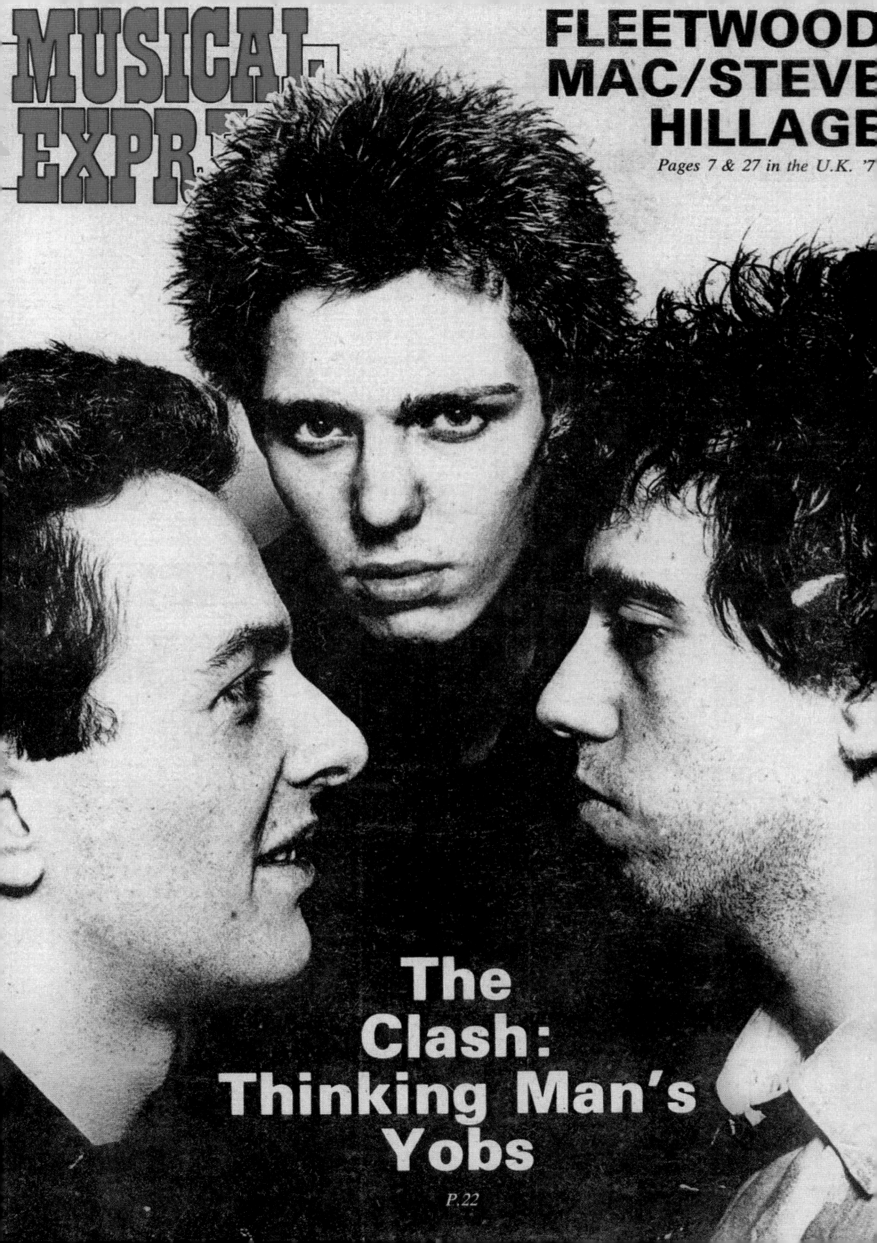

MUSICAL EXPR

FLEETWOOD MAC/STEVE HILLAGE

Pages 7 & 27 in the U.K. '7

The Clash: Thinking Man's Yobs

P.22

CALVIN HAYES

I first met legendary guitarist Chris Spedding in late 1972 when he began working with my father, Mickie Most, on Donovan's *Cosmic Wheels* album. He subsequently became his go to session guitarist. Although they had entirely opposing life styles, they liked and respected each other.

In the summer of '75, Chris played a song to my father that he'd written called 'Motor Bikin.' Seeing as my father loved motorbikes, he thought the song had a shot. They duly recorded it and the single was a fairly big hit. It was a commercial, raw, yet tight throwback to the fifties with a killer guitar solo. It was very out of step for the time as was Chris with his rocker image and slicked-back hair which was all deeply unfashionable. Nevertheless, I thought he was dead cool.

Chris's performance of 'Motor Bikin' on *Top Of The Pops* in August that year, while wearing Let It Rock clothes, made an impression on a young group called the Sex Pistols. As Steve Jones and Paul Cook were Roxy Music fans, they were well of aware of Chris and his involvement with Bryan Ferry, particularly his stellar playing on the 'Price of Love.' Glen Matlock had also met him in '74 while working as a Saturday boy at Let It Rock where Chris bought a lot of his clothes that were tailored by Malcolm McLaren and Vivienne Westwood.

Shortly after, Chris started dating an American journalist called Chrissie Hynde, who was part of the embryonic Punk scene. She and a young drummer called Chris Miller (later known as Rat Scabies) took Chris to the Sex Pistols performance at London's 100 Club at the end of March '76.

The band nearly imploded on stage that night, their singer Johnny Rotten refusing to join the band for an encore.

At the end, Rotten was introduced to Spedding and he told Chris he was fed up working with the group and was considering leaving because, as far as he was concerned, they were going nowhere. Chris told him that they were great and he was onto a good thing.

A little later, when I was 12 years-old, during a break at Morgan Studios for one of the *Motor Bikin'* album sessions, I was complaining to Chris about the bland musical scene. He told me he'd seen this new young band and they were the future of rock and roll. I remember he was very animated and enthusiastic at the time and didn't notice he was spilling some of his pint down his shirt. So, I made a mental note, the Sex Pistols.

The Pistols hadn't recorded any demos at that point so Chris agreed to produce one for free, which they did on 15 May 1976, at Majestic Studios, a cinema converted into a 24-track studio off Clapham High Road. My father always assumed he'd paid for it and it turned out to be true.

The three-track demo comprised the songs Chris considered their strongest; 'Problems', 'No Feelings' and 'Pretty Vacant' ('Anarchy in the UK' and 'God Save the Queen' hadn't been written at that point).

Early one evening I was in my bedroom listening to some music when my father burst in wearing his black Lewis leathers' motorbike gear (he'd just driven home on his Norton from the RAK office in Charles Street). He seemed a little agitated.

"Spedding's been bending my ear about this group called the Sex Pistols. I can't make head nor tail of it. What do you think?" he asked and chucked a cassette tape in my direction.

Initially, the rhythm section appeared fairly traditional, but a little stripped down, edgy and spiky. I remember being shocked at how raw and unpolished the vocals sounded. And what lyrics I could make out, really struck a nerve with me. Totally honest, cutting and direct. My favourite song was 'Pretty Vacant'. I couldn't believe that the singer was clearly singing "Va..cunt." There also wasn't the slightest hint of Americanism in his vocal delivery either.

A couple of days later, my father and I were driving somewhere together. I'd bought the cassette, which I'd been listening to nonstop, and told him he should absolutely, definitely sign

them. He told me to put it on again so he could check it out.

After listening to it together we were both convinced that Spedding had played the lead guitar parts... which is a great compliment to Steve Jones.

He then proceeded to have an unproductive meeting with the group's obnoxious manager, Malcolm McLaren, at the bar of the Hilton Hotel in Hyde Park. For some strange reason, McLaren insisted they met there instead of his office in Dryden Chambers around the corner from Charles Street.

Having been round the block a few times, my father could see exactly what Malcolm was up to – he was doing what Andrew Loog Oldham had done with the Stones in the sixties. That was fine by him; he certainly wasn't averse to a bit of publicity, good or bad. But what put the mockers on it was Malcolm's arrogance. He insisted that if RAK wanted to sign the band, they had to ditch their stable of pop acts, such as Smokie and Hot Chocolate who were selling millions of records. Understandably, my father passed.

However, that didn't stop me pestering him about the Pistols as I followed their rise in the music press and we had many, many rows about it. My cousin Johnathan and I even jokingly offered to regularly wash his cars – and he had a few – in return for signing them. But it was not to be.

When, EMI eventually did sign them – and promptly dropped them as did A&M weeks later – the issue kept rearing its ugly head. I did correctly foresee that Richard Branson would embrace the concept and clean up by signing them to Virgin and help secure so many future new wave and post Punk acts who would end up selling internationally.

"Punk won't sell south of Dover Hoverport," was my father's response when I ribbed him. In a sense, he was correct at the time, though the long-term, cultural significance of the Punk movement has proven to be immense. Although it did feel like the world was truly changing and a movement was growing in 1976, I never thought in a million years I'd be contributing to a book on Punk all these years later. Look how long Punk took to really take off, even in the States. Twenty years?

During a trip to LA in late 1977 with my parents, I snuck out to the Whiskey a Go Go on Sunset Strip to see The Ramones and The Runaways; not a bad double bill. God knows how I got in, I was supposed to be 21. I was shocked to see 150 people, at most, when I did. They weren't terribly excited either. In London, at the time, there'd be thousands pogoing away.

Anyway, that Pistols demo was my introduction to Punk, which I believe hadn't even been termed that when I heard it over six months prior to the release of 'Anarchy in the UK'.

DAVID MCDONALD

Being 12 years old, I was a bit of a fan of Queen at the time and had seen some very small mentions in the press of something called "Punk Rock". It really didn't appeal to me at first. I wondered if Queen would turn punk to join in with this new fad. Didn't really hear or see anything more about it until the Bill Grundy interview, after which, the papers were full of it.

Those pictures in the press were really the first time I had properly seen the Sex Pistols and what they looked like. I was impressed. I suppose it seemed a bit of a dressing up game to annoy people. There wasn't much music to buy at that point and it wasn't until a bit later on, probably early '77, when I first heard 'Anarchy In The UK' at a mate's house. I thought it was great, but I thought 'I Wanna Be Me' was even better. I can't lie and say I had an epiphany moment, but I was impressed enough to be interested in this whole punk thing. I think it slowly grew from there.

I'm sure it was different living in London at the time, but in Dundee there weren't many gigs, and the ones that did happen were in licensed venues so you really had to be 18 to get in. It was really buying the odd record and customising clothes that was the main thing for me.

It was only a few years later when anyone you knew was going to London, you'd give them some cash to buy you a t-shirt or muslin top from Seditionaries, or some pointed creepers from Robot. *A Day At The Races* was the last record I ever bought by Queen!

My favourite punk song changes from time to time, but I think I'll opt for The Clash - 'Complete Control' and Buzzcocks - 'Orgasm Addict'. Both have great record sleeves too. I think another great thing about punk was the artwork of the 7" single.

Jumpers - Hand knitted by my Mum.

Shirt - Second hand shirt probably bought from Oxfam or a jumble sale. I traced letters from a newspaper for writing on breast aided by a glass coffee table and lamp to make seeing the letters easier. Coloured in with felt tip laundry markers. 'Spunk' was written in red shoe dye with the dye applicator. This was made either the tail end of '77 or early '78.

Anarchy t-shirt - Contrary to what most people thought, it wasn't made from a pillow case. I found some thin white material at home and thought it would be ideal to trace some Sex Pistols artwork as I couldn't afford to buy one, or know where to get one if I had the money. I copied the Anarchy poster which was in a book and added the logo and 'Bollocks to EMI' to it to give it a different look. Outlined all of it with a biro laundry marker, then coloured it in with indelible felt pens. Front and back were hand sewn together. Again, this was made either the tail end of '77 or early '78. It's too difficult to remember exactly when, but it was definitely post *Never Mind the Bollocks*. Subsequently signed by Malcolm Owen of the Ruts when they played Dundee University in '79 or '80.

The rest of the items were bought around '79-'81 from trips to London.

MIKE PICKLES

In 1975 I was 16 and just starting 'A' levels. I lived in Leeds and times were grim. No future for us was a reality, not a punk song still waiting to be written.

I first learnt about the Punk scene in London from my father's copies of the *News of the World* and the *Daily Mirror*. At that stage I thought my flares were much better than the tight trousers the punks wore.

Leeds then was an uninteresting place to be. Ok, we were only 16, but underage drinking seemed to be normal. You were considered to like good music if you went to the Precinct pub where, at the start of the week, the music was split between David Bowie and Roxy Music with half-hour blasts of each. We danced many a night away but it was pub closing at 10:30pm and off for the last bus home at 11:05pm. We had no extra money for taxis, so missing the last bus was not an option.

There was increasing mention of the punk thing so, out of curiosity, when The Clash played the Queens Hall in 1977, I went along with a bunch of mates including Tim, Howard and our Brian. I remember Nicky Clarkson also coming along and he wore a pyjama top. I was very impressed with his dress sense. Before the gig, we went to the Scarborough Taps pub nearby where I saw my first real punk girl and she was showing her breasts just like the punk girls did in the *News of the World.*

Maybe that's what got me into punk.

We heard on the grapevine that the Queen's Hall had a no drinks license, so we loaded up with cans hidden in our clothing and went to the concert. Our beers were soon discovered at the entry search so we spent a further quarter of an hour outside drinking our contraband. No way were we going to discard unopened cans of beer.

My only recollection is that I don't remember anything about the songs or music. But I had a great time.

A few weeks later, The Ramones played Leeds University. Tim and I went to see them and that's when I knew I would be a punk forever.

For me, Punk in the UK was a protest movement and rebellion against the lack of opportunity. The backdrop to all this was the music and fashion. Punk has never died. It showed that just because you had nothing it didn't mean you had to accept it. Why not give it a go? If you've got nothing, you've got nothing to lose. God bless Malcolm McLaren for giving us hope and all who went along with the punk movement.

HO ARE THE

Sex Pistol on murder charge

UNDER ARREST . . . Sid Vicious is led away to jail by a New York detective under the glare of cameramen's flash lights.

SID VICIOUS 'KNIFES GIRL TO DEATH'

Johnny Rotten . . . he was fined £40 for possessing a drug.

THINK . . . U.S.A

THE FILTH AND THE FURY!

Bored Stiff.
TILL '77! Nº1

WITH . . .
SEX PISTOLS
PENETRATION
JAM
TUBES
& OTHER FADS

One Night Only — AT THE 'COLISEUM' Cinema MANOR PK ROAD HARL

PROGRAMME
7.00pm — 11.00
GROUPS
11.15 — ONWA
Uncensored
KUNG-FU
FILMS

FRIDAY 11th MARCH
THE CLASH
BUZZ COCKS
Subway +
the Sect +
Slits +
LATE NIGHT
KUNG-FU
FILMS

HERE

Admission £1.50

Sex Pistols lose
battle
to beat
U.S. ban

ROSIE MELLOWS

I was asked (by a gorgeous lad) if I liked Punk at a club in North London and realized that I didn't know anything about it. I hadn't heard any, there were no records. My mate and I decided to find out. I think I went to my first gig at the 100 Club.

I made friends through Punk. I re-met an old friend recently who I hadn't seen for over 34 years and when we met it was like we'd seen each other only a couple of weeks ago.

I'm still making friends through Punk. The scene is very much alive. I go to many gigs throughout the year, and the Rebellion festival is a standout.

My favourite gig back then was an Ants one at the London College of Printing. I was a bit tipsy that night and I asked someone where the loos were, they pointed and said, "Up there" (maybe they said "Out there" but it was noisy and thought I heard "Up") so I went up the stairs and up again, and eventually came to a door – but it was to the roof. I heard some noise and walked to the edge of the roof and looked down to see a row of quiffs surrounding the college, who were in turn surrounded by the little shiny bits on the top of police helmets. At the end of the gig all the Punks got a police escort down to the tube station – we were given no option, we had to go to the tube – I think they were trying to prevent a huge fight. I also remember there was a bit of a fire on stage that night. It all added to the atmosphere.

One night I met a friend and got on a bus near my house. My mum got on at the next stop. I said hello but she ignored me and walked straight past. It was ok to talk to me indoors, but she wouldn't acknowledge us in public. So, I paid her fare and said in a loud voice "Three tickets please, that for me, my mate and my Mum, the woman in the brown coat and the perm. That's my Mum." The woman sitting in the row between us said to her, "Ooh she looks just like you, love." When we got to the stop by the tube station, Mum got off first and waited for us at the stop. She said to me, "It's less embarrassing to be seen with you than to try and ignore you!"

When you were out in public, people would shy away from you. I pretended not to notice but inside I'd be laughing, thinking, why are you reacting like that? It's just clothes.

I read some fanzines, the *NME* and *Melody Maker*, and for several years practically lived in the Music Machine thanks to the free tickets and half price tickets given away most nights, along with it being on the N29 bus route (when I lived with Mum and Dad) and being just a walk to the Kings Cross squats.

I went to the Music Machine, the Electric Ballroom, the 100 Club, the Marquee, the Lyceum, the Nashville, the Moonlight Club, the Hope and Anchor, the Bridge House and many other places, names I've forgotten.

Before Punk, I think I was a labour supporter mainly due to my Dad's outlook on life. It was only through The Clash that I started to take notice of politics. I'm still a 'leftie'

Rock Against Racism was important to me as I have always been anti-racist and some of the gigs were pretty damn good.

Punk after 1978 tended to be a little more uniform. Bands seemed more likely to follow a stricter formula, but I didn't mind much.

I have many Punk songs that I love, 'New Rose' The Damned, 'White Riot' and 'White Man In Hammersmith Palais' The Clash, 'Don't Dictate' Penetration, 'Where Were You?' The Mekons, 'Cranked Up Really High' Slaughter and the Dogs, 'Rockers' Stranglehold and 'Warhead' UK Subs.

There were many good bands that didn't make it, like The Straps. They're still going and I go and see them wh enever I can.

I loved my leather jacket, which was given to me by Garry. I wish I still had it, I don't know where it went.

My clothes came from all over the place. I made some, had some bits from Boy although I couldn't afford much. I think I had some bondage trousers and a mohair, some bits from The Last Resort

which was around the corner from my day release college and where me and my friend spent most lunch hours as most of the people on my course at college wouldn't speak to us because we were Punks. We also shopped in second hand/charity shops. Mick (?), the owner of the shop, used to make us coffee. I think he liked us hanging round the shop and free coffee when you were on day release was always a good thing. We bought jeans from anywhere. All the jeans you could get then were flares but my mate Garry's nan used to take them in and turn them into drainpipes.

I sometimes wore a black leather miniskirt and fishnets with winkle pickers. I don't know that I was thinking of looking attractive, I was just into having fun, listening to bands, and dressing outrageously for the time. I went out with Garry Orange for a long time who was in the Spotty Dogs and had played The Roxy. He used to sing 'New Rose' to me, I think that was quite romantic! Before Garry, I had the odd crush on people, and usually just chatted them up. Sometimes it led to more, sometimes not.

I had no hopes for Punk, it was just immediate and of the moment. But that 'moment' has lasted a bloody long time for me. Not that I'm complaining. It did break down a lot of barriers. People started to ignore the 'correct way' to get music released and started to do it for themselves. Before Punk I was a quiet girl, but I went to my first gig and that changed me almost immediately. I'd found a music and a lifestyle I loved. My biggest regret was that I didn't get into Punk earlier and I missed out on going to The Roxy.

I remember going home once and my Mum looked at me, gave a theatrical shudder and said, "Yeughhh! Look at you. I thought if I ignored you long enough you'd grow out of it. BUT YOU HAVEN'T! I have visions of you looking like that when you're a grandmother." Mum, you were so right. I'm not a grandmother, but I'm old enough to be!

STEVE CARVER

Woking 1976.

Two things happened to me during that long hot Summer, Paul Weller moved into the house at the bottom of my garden and I discovered Punk Rock.

Before that…

England was grey. Woking was dead.

At a loose end one day, I wandered into my local pub and spotted my new neighbour at the bar. I nodded and we started talking. Paul told me he was in a band and within minutes he mentioned the Sex Pistols, "Have you seen them yet…?"

I hadn't, but I had been following their progress in the music press. I had seen the pic of them 'beating up their audience', and knew I had to check this group out. "A bunch of us are going to see 'em on Tuesday," said Paul. "Come with us…"

"Don't look over your shoulder, but the Sex Pistols are coming."

The 100 Club, London. Sex Pistols /The Clash.

1976. No YouTube. No Spotify. You had to and go see a 'Live Band' if you wanted to know what all the fuss was about.

I entered the basement club with my new mates. It was full of people our age. The atmosphere was electric. Strummer and Jones were drinking at the bar. In the crowd I spotted Johnny Rotten, his knees were tied together and it looked like he had hacked at his hair and clothes with the same pair of scissors. As I watched, a girl attached a crucifix to his jacket with a safety pin.

He clambered onstage with his band and fixed the audience with that 'Rotten' stare. You couldn't take your eyes off him. "GET OFF YOU'RE ARSES!" Straight into 'Anarchy In The UK…'

The place erupted. It was instant. The crowd surged, pushing, shoving, pogoing. It was more like a football crowd than a rock concert…

This was a different planet from Alice Cooper at Wembley or Bowie at Hammersmith. A million miles from Woking…

Before that day I had never heard a note of what the *NME* had labelled 'PUNK ROCK'. But the Pistols (and The Clash) sounded exactly as I expected. The attitude, the anger, the Raw Power. But more than that, it was the connection to the audience. AT LAST, a band that was talking to ME. It all made sense. I loved it!!! That night, I would have swapped my entire record collection for just one Sex Pistols' album.

The next day one of my 'straight' mates down the pub asked, "But it's not proper music, is it? "Nah," I said. "It's much better than that…!!!!"

It didn't take a genius to work out that the Punk Rock/new wave 'movement' was the perfect audience for The JAM. The same energy, passion, 'fire and skill'.

And they grabbed it with both hands …

The next year or so became a blur of pubs, clubs and gigs. The 'Woking Contingent' became regulars on the scene. The JAM became the hardest working band in London. It seemed we were in Soho every weekend either playing a gig or just hanging out. I must have seen the JAM play 100 times in 76 -77.

Every venue from Soho Open Market (very early doors on a Saturday lunchtime with The Clash checking 'em out), The Marquee, 100 Club, Roxy, Vortex, Nashville, Hope & Anchor, Red Cow, and even Ronnie Scott's (the famous jazz club). Most of these places were dark, damp, dingy, dangerous, sinister and secretive and I couldn't get enough. I would scan the gig-guide and plan my weekend. If it was a JAM gig, we would make the journey home in the back of a Transit van, drunk, sweaty, exhausted, with Paul's dad, the wonderful John Weller at the wheel. If not, we would jump the train and suss out that week's climber.

Most Saturdays we would miss the last train home to Woking, catch the milk express at 3am and walk home just as the morning sun was rising...

I look back on those days with immense happiness. I feel extremely lucky to be somehow 'part of it', privileged to be in the eye of the storm, so to speak.

Sometimes (once in a lifetime), you are in the right place at the right time. I was that soldier and I wouldn't have missed it for the world...

The funny thing was, back in 1977 everyone had to pretend to be 'bored out of their minds'. Truth was, we were all having an absolute blast.

"Didn't we have a nice time, wasn't it such a fine time…"

STEVE PARISH

I have two memories of 1976 – sitting in our in tiny back garden in Forest Hill sweltering in the hottest summer on record, and watching the *Today* programme on 1 December aged 11. Even now it would be pretty shocking to hear a band cursing and swearing away before the watershed, but then it caused an eruption that reverberated around the country even though *Today* only aired in London. I suppose it wasn't just the words but the contemptuous way they were uttered at such an established, often grumpy, straight-laced figure like Bill Grundy on such a generally innocuous show.

I heard Billy Bragg once say that if he had a pound for everyone that saw The Clash at The Roundhouse in 1976 he'd be a rich man, I hadn't even heard of Punk until that broadcast and anyone of my age that says they had is probably taking nonsense. But from that moment I'd found my music. I had no truck with disco and up to that point I didn't mind listening to a bit of Elvis.

I love a lyric, a sentiment, some anger and a point of view with a hard-edged melody! The first discovery was that, contrary to their portrayal, the Pistols could play and once they had laid the ground others followed. I couldn't get enough of it. Still if you asked me for my favourite Punk record I would say Eddie and the Hot Rods, 'Do Anything You Wanna Do'. No band or record sums up what Punk meant more – when they weren't playing they could be robbing banks. I'm amazed it isn't played more now. Such a great record.

From '77 the refinement of Punk took me through The Clash and The Damned, listening to and often recording John Peel illicitly under the covers listening to his great introductions. Many of the records got banned. I remember Peel saying of 'Smash It Up' that presumably it was banned on some stations because if young people listened to it they might go and raze whole cities to the ground!

1977 saw the release of 'Rat Trap' and every word was learnt, the same for 'I Don't Like Mondays'. Britain was a shocking, strike-ridden, filthy place frankly and the lyrics of 'Rat Trap' told me

everything you didn't want to be while Eddie and the Rods screamed go and make what you want happen. The day I turned down the job in insurance, a turning point in my life that led to a completely fulfilling career in first advertising and then sport, was directly attributable to these sentiments.

1982 and we all followed the Jam into the Style Council mainly because they had more girls following them. At the Dominion in '83, the support act was a guy with a guitar, a big nose and a load of chat who took to the stage and enthused a crowd of post Punk soulboys and girls. It was a complete epiphany for me and the very epitome of Punk. "Weller told me, 'Bill you gotta tune that guitar son.'" Pause as Billy Bragg looks at the tuning machine the very same had donated to the cause and then bang, "I don't want to change the world, I'm not looking for a new England, I'm just looking for another girl."

Life's A Riot with Spy Vs Spy – the single best Punk, post Punk, Punk inspired album ever. I left for holiday the day after that Dominion gig and it never came off my Walkman. Billy performs it as an encore. For the uninitiated reader, Billy's a sort of opinionated, rough round the edges Ed Sheeran. Through the eighties and nineties he lived his life three or four years ahead of mine and his songs reflected my life. Can't get a job? Listen to 'To Have And To Have Not'. Can't get a girl? Listen to 'Saturday Boy.' Lost your girl? Then you

LIFE'S A RIOT
WITH SPY VS SPY

BILLY BRAGG

30TH ANNIVERSARY EDITION

30TH ANNIVERSARY EDITION

30th
REMASTERED
ORIGINAL
& EXCLUSIVE
LIVE VERSION
Anniversary
Edition

need the whole of *Workers Playtime*. My pride and joy is his 'Happy Birthday' message to me on my 50th. I wonder if songwriters and singers ever really know what their songs mean to people? Maybe I'm the only person that thinks his cover of 'Tracks Of My Tears' edges Smokey's version. Give it a listen.

Later years – Blink 182 with my daughter at Wembley on their last tour; Green Day in Brighton, simply the best live band I've ever seen (Punk doesn't come on at midnight anymore and tell the audience that's been waiting four hours to fuck off); chatting to Richard Jobson of that great band The Skids in the Groucho about the old days

Punk's influence will never leave me or any of us. Thank God for that!

SEX PISTOLS

TUES 15th

100 CLUB
100 OXFORD ST, W1

sartorial
correctness

Sex Pistols

and a CASt (PLAStER)

7.30 till LAtE. bars

CONTRIBUTORS...

INTRODUCTION...

Nicky Weller, Barry Cain, Russell Reader...

NEVER MIND THE BOLLOCKS...

Joe Corre...	Co-Founder of Agent Provocateur

ANARCHY IN THE UK...

Andy Radwan (Blade)...	Eater
Andy McCluskey...	Orchestral Manoeuvres In The Dark
Billy Bragg...	Singer/Songwriter
Billy Idol...	Generation X
Debbie Harry...	Blondie
Boz Boorer...	The Polecats, Morrissey
Bruce Foxton...	The Jam
Captain Sensible...	The Damned
Carl Hunter...	The Farm
Chris Difford...	Squeeze
Clem Burke...	Blondie
Dave Parsons...	Sham 69
Debsey Wykes...	Dolly Mixture
Duncan 'Kid' Reid...	The Boys
Ed Bazalgette...	The Vapors
John 'Eddie' Edwards...	The Vibrators
Gaye Black...	The Adverts
Glen Matlock...	Sex Pistols, Rich Kids
Hazel O'Connor...	Singer
Hugh Cornwell...	The Stranglers
Iggy Pop...	Singer
Jean-Jacques Burnel...	The Stranglers
Joe Strummer...	The Clash
John Ellis...	The Vibrators
Jennie Bellestar...	The Bellestars
John Lydon...	Sex Pistols, P.I.L.
Jordan Mooney...	Punk Icon
Johnny Thunders...	The Heartbreakers
Kym Bradshaw...	The Saints
Matt Dangerfield...	The Boys
Mick Jones...	The Clash, Big Audio Dynamite
Paul Weller...	The Jam
Pauline Murray...	Penetration
Pete Holidai...	Radiators From Space
Peter Hooton...	The Farm
Poly Styrene...	X ray Specs
Rat Scabies...	The Damned
Rhoda Dakar...	The Bodysnatchers
Rick Buckler...	The Jam
Rusty Egan...	The Rich Kids
Shirley Manson...	Garbage
Steve Brookes...	Founding member of The Jam
Steve Diggle...	The Buzzcocks
Steve Ellis...	Love Affair
Steve Rapid...	Radiators From Space
Steve Sidelnyk...	Primal Scream
Toyah	Singer
Tom Verlaine	Television

COMPLETE CONTROL...

Alan Edwards...	PR consultant
Alan McGee...	Creation Records
Andrew Czezowski & Susan Carrington...	The Roxy Club Founders
Bill Smith...	Graphic Designer
Chris Parry...	A&R man that signed The Jam for Polydor
Frank Warren...	Boxing Promoter
Malcolm McLaren...	Sex Pistols Manager
Nigel House...	Rough Trade
Sean Forbes...	Rough Trade

GABBA GABBA HEY!...

Don Letts...	DJ and film maker
Eddie Piller...	Acid Jazz, DJ
Gary Crowley...	Radio DJ
Mike Read...	Radio DJ

SOMETHING BETTER CHANGE...

Fred Armisen...	Actor and Comedian
Graham Fellows aka Jilted John...	Comedian
Martin Freeman...	Actor & Hobbit

NEAT NEAT NEAT...